Why *Daily Handwriting Practice?*

The premise behind *Daily Handwriting Practice* is simple and straightforward—frequent, focused practice of a skill leads to mastery and retention of that skill.

What's in *Daily Handwriting Practice?*

The book is divided into 36 weekly sections. Practice for Monday through Thursday includes half pages on which students practice writing letters, words, and sentences. Friday's practice involves a full page.

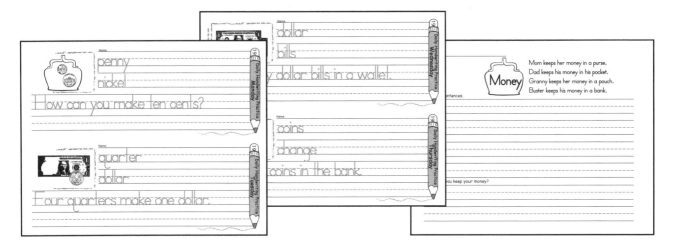

Daily Handwriting Practice is more than handwriting.

Students are practicing a variety of important vocabulary words:

color words	months
number words—cardinal and ordinal	sports
verbs	position words
animal names	family members
days of the week	

As they write and read words in context, students are learning about curriculum topics:

nutrition	the continents
the solar system	geometric shapes
the layers of the earth	money
recycling	energy
fractions	

Letter
Formation Chart

Aa Bb Cc Dd

Ee Ff Gg Hh

Ii Jj Kk Ll

Mm Nn Oo Pp

Qq Rr Ss Tt

Uu Vv Ww Xx

Yy Zz

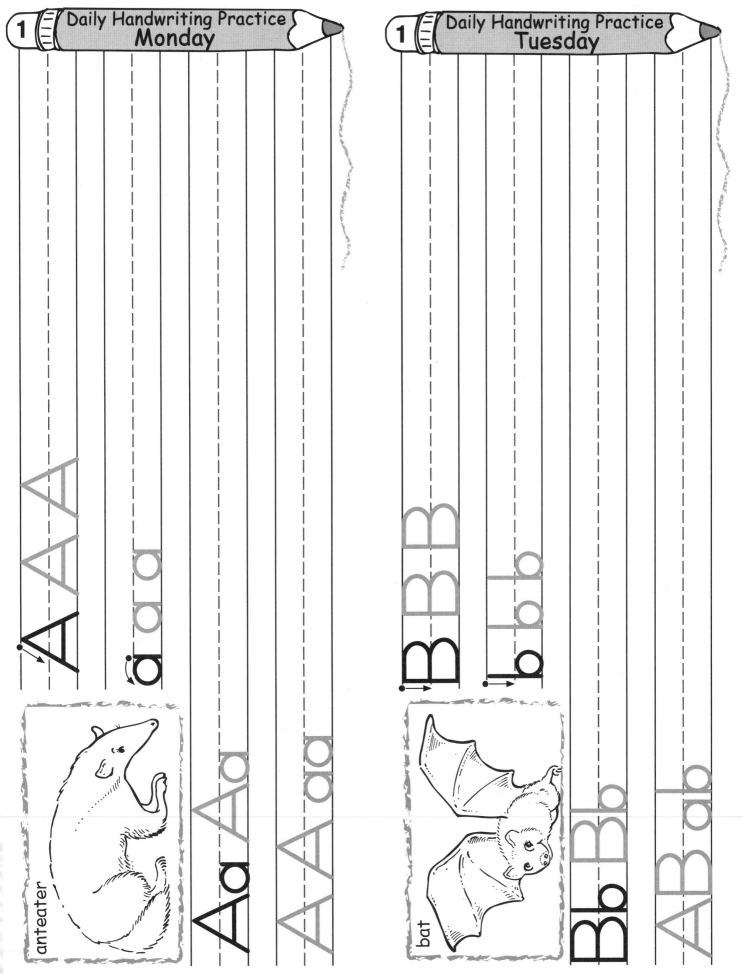

anteater

bat

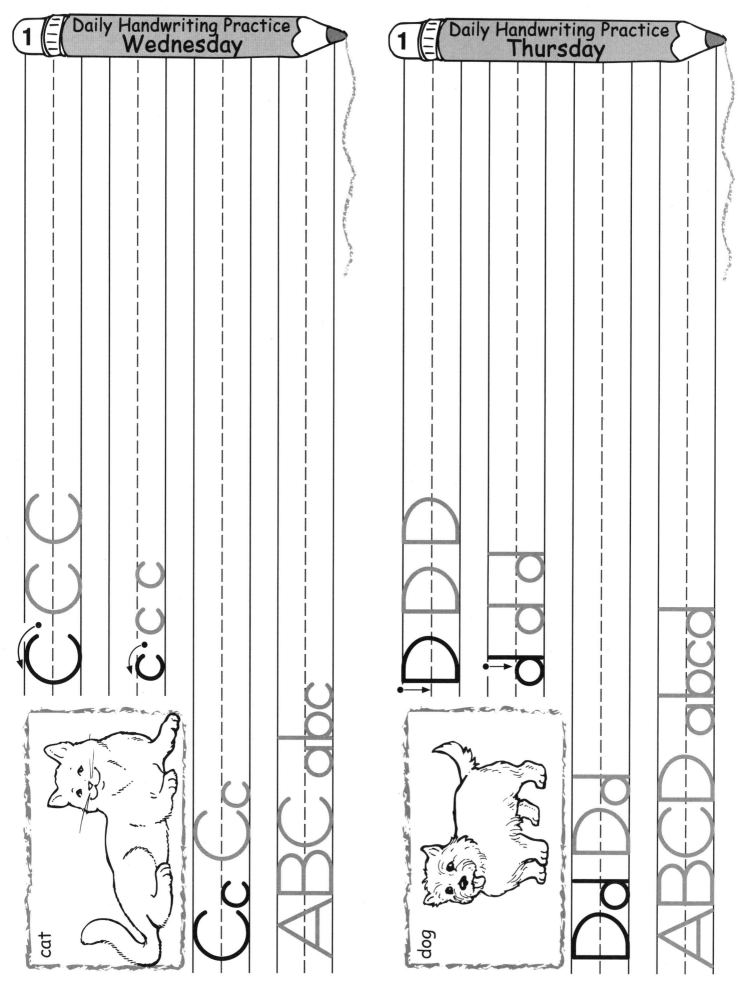

Cc Cc

ABC abc

cat

Dd Dd

ABCD abcd

dog

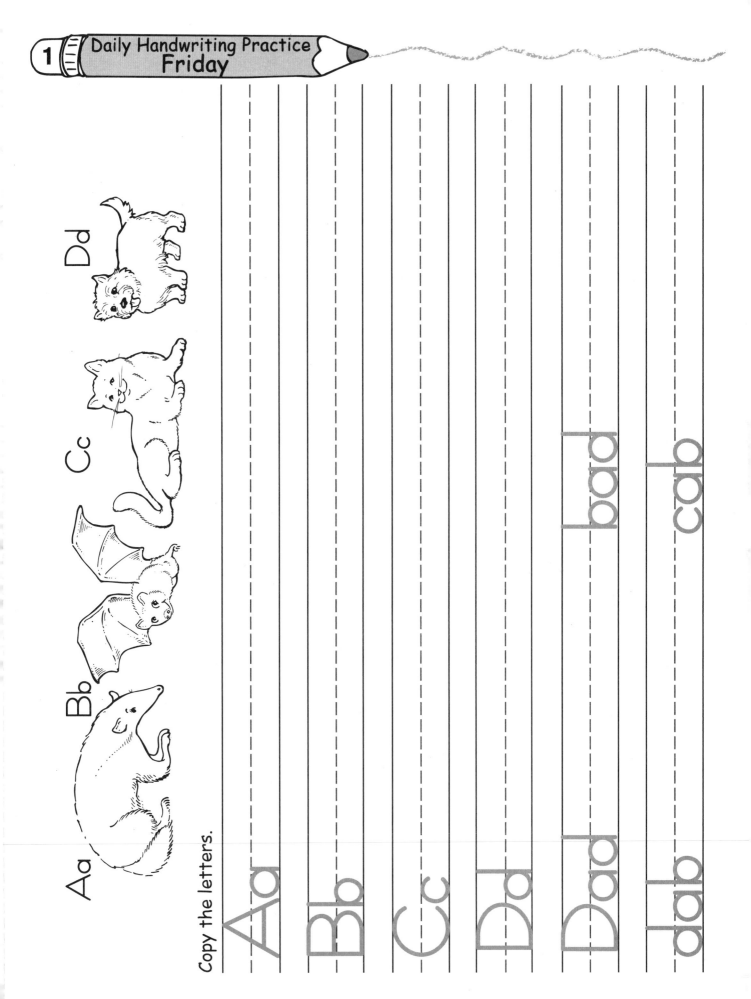

Aa   Bb   Cc   Dd

Copy the letters.

Aa

Bb

Cc

Dd

Dad   bad

dab   cab

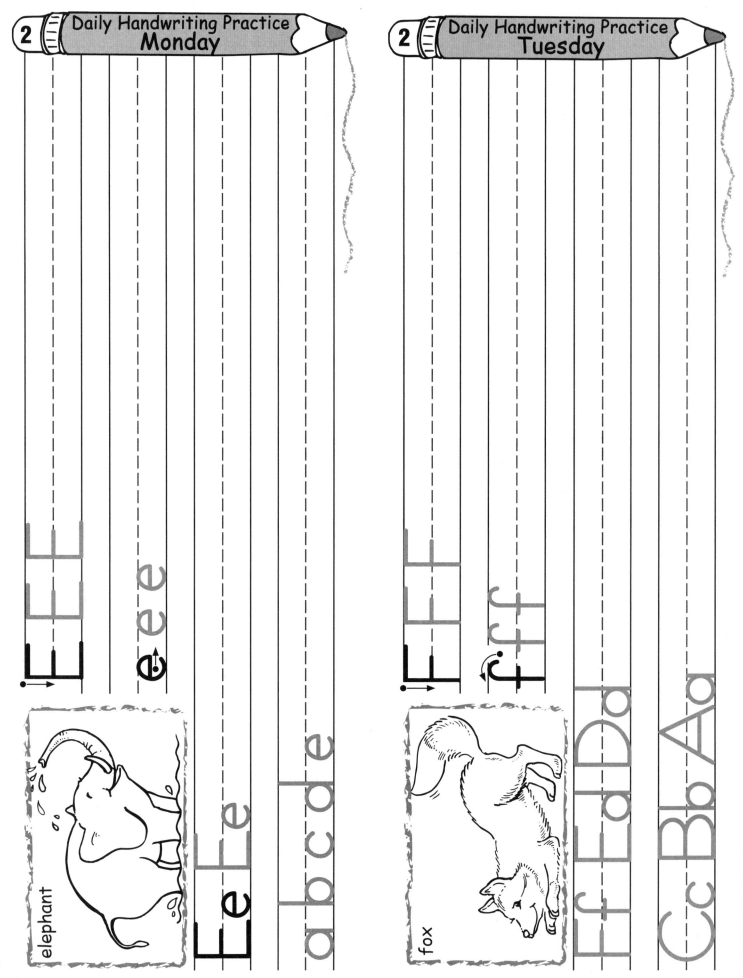

E E E

e e e

E e E e

a b c d e

elephant

F F F

f f f

F f E d D d

C c B b A a

fox

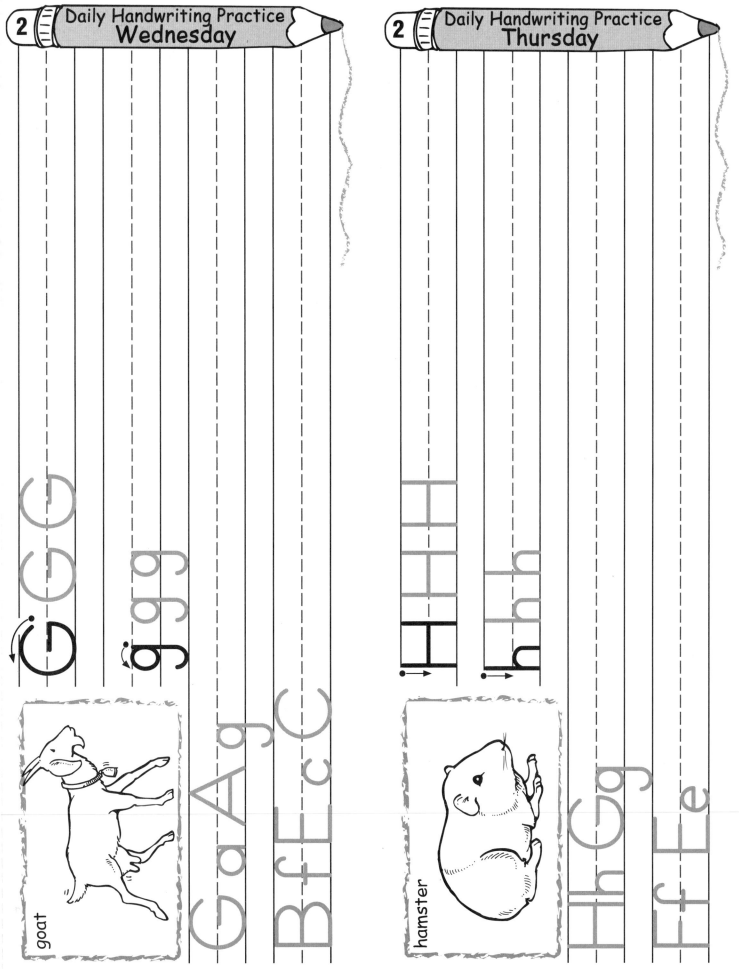

goat

hamster

Trace and write.

egg

bag

bead

cab

head

bed

Match It Up

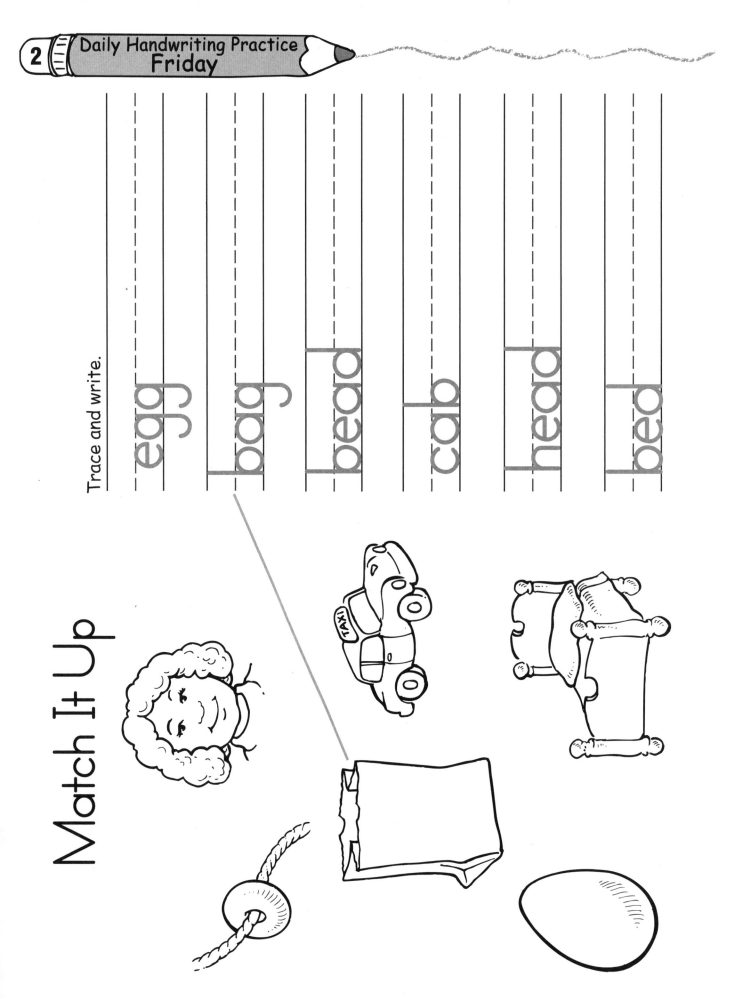

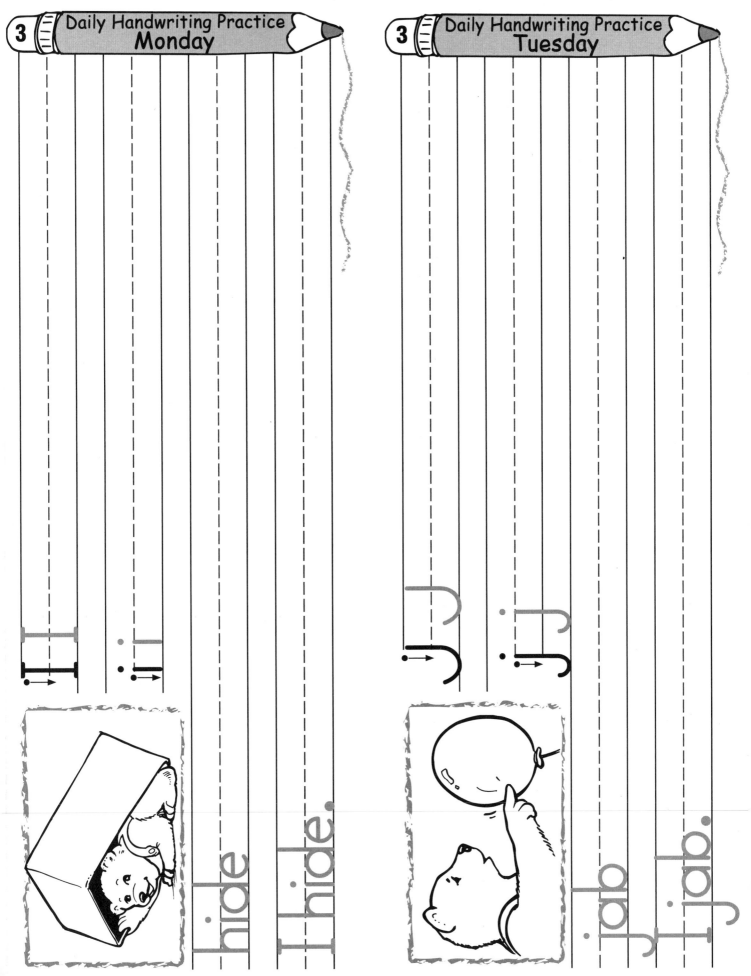

I i

.i hide

I hide.

J j

j jab

J jab.

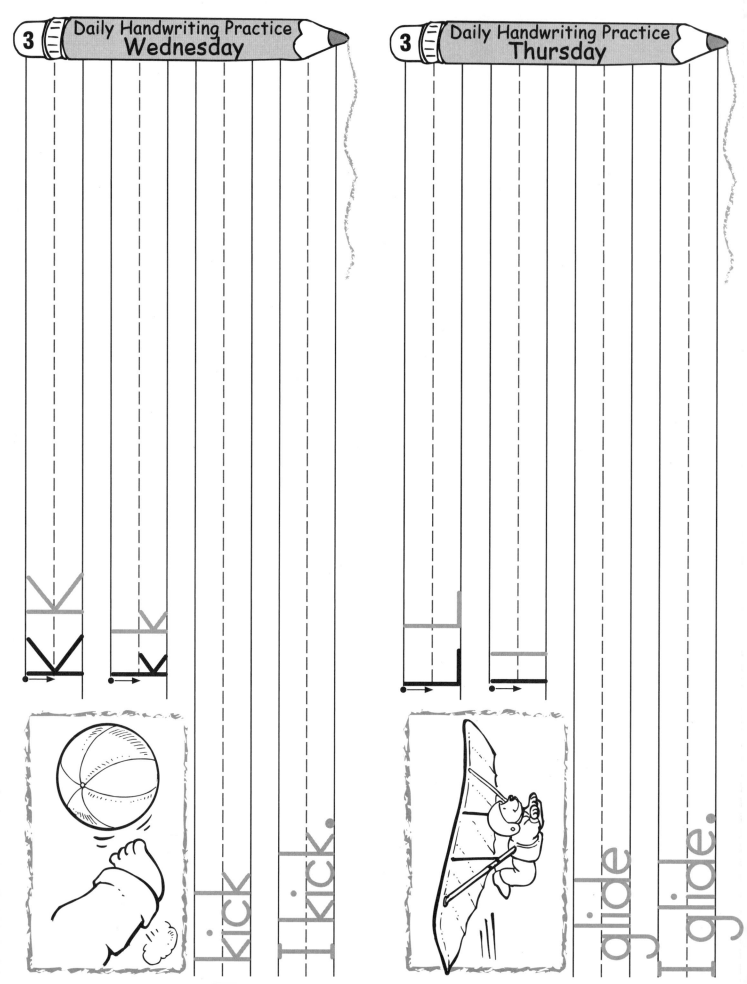

kick

I kick.

glide

I glide.

Things I Can Do

Trace and write.

I hide.

I kick.

I glide.

I jab.

I lace.

I dig.

I beg.

4 Daily Handwriting Practice Monday

M M

m m

Mmmm mmmm!

I like cake.

4 Daily Handwriting Practice Tuesday

N N

n n

Nice!

Neckties are nice.

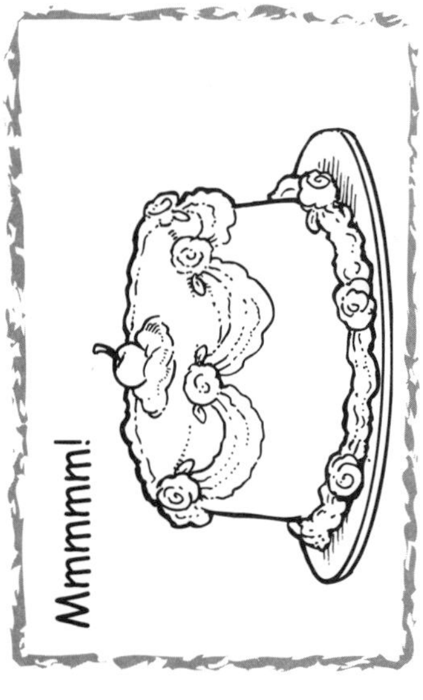

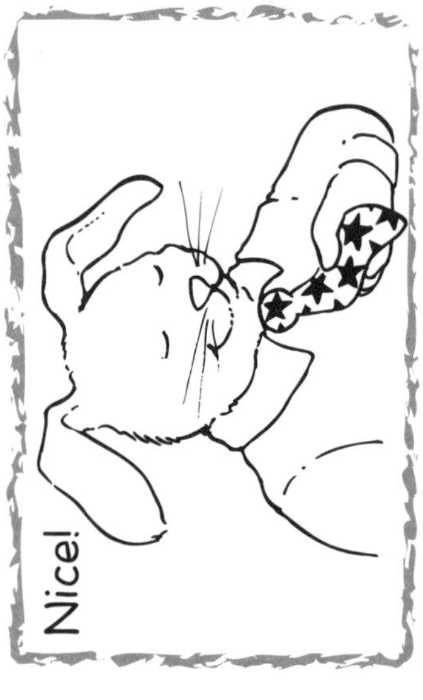

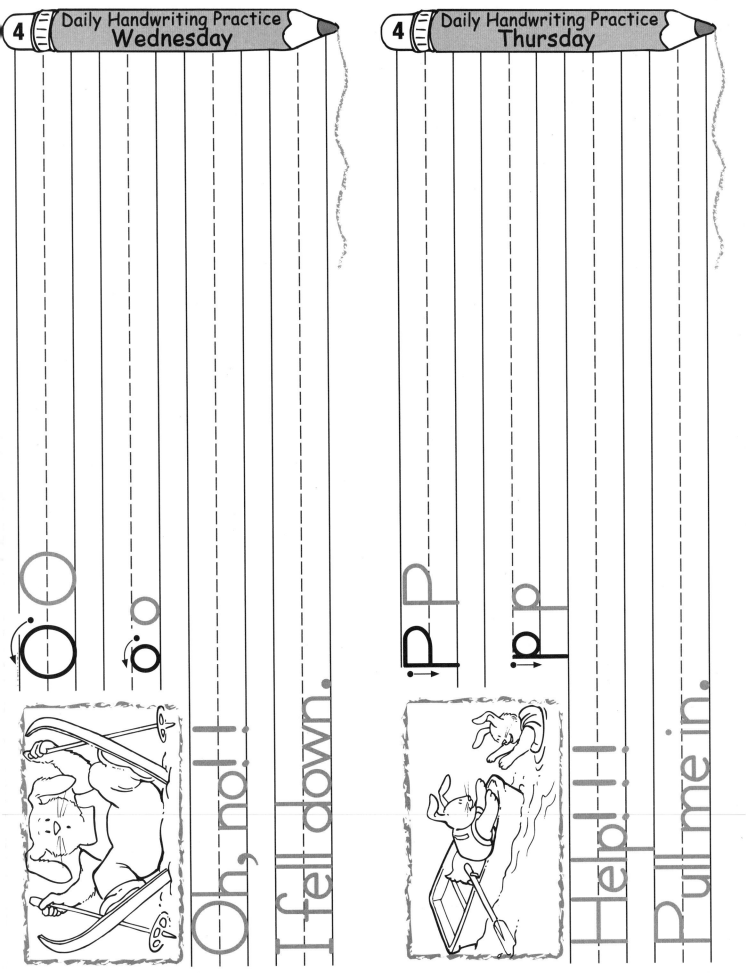

O O

o o

Oh, no!

I fell down.

P P

p p

Help!!!

Pull me in.

13

Ben Digs

Can Ben find a map?
Can Ben find a bone?

Can Ben find a map?

Dig, Ben, Dig.
Dig deep.
Find a bone.

Good job, Ben.

Qq

Qq

Quack, quack.

Rr

Rr

Roar. Grrrrr!

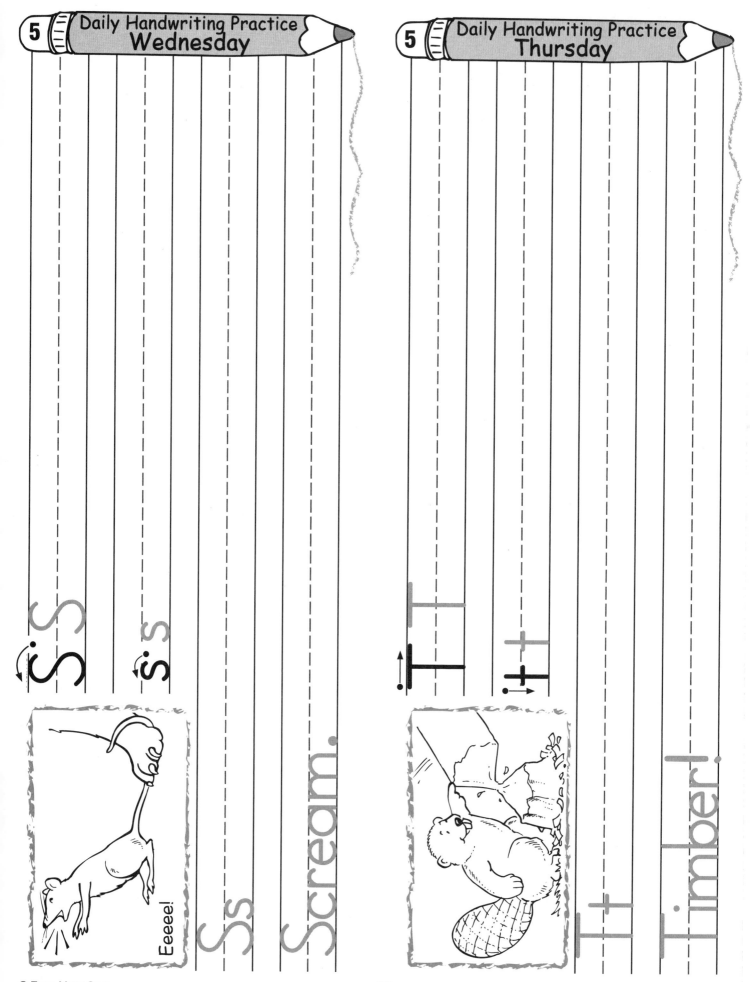

Ss

Ss

Eeeee!

Ss

Scream.

Tt

Tt

Tt

Timber!

Make a wish
for a fish
on a dish.

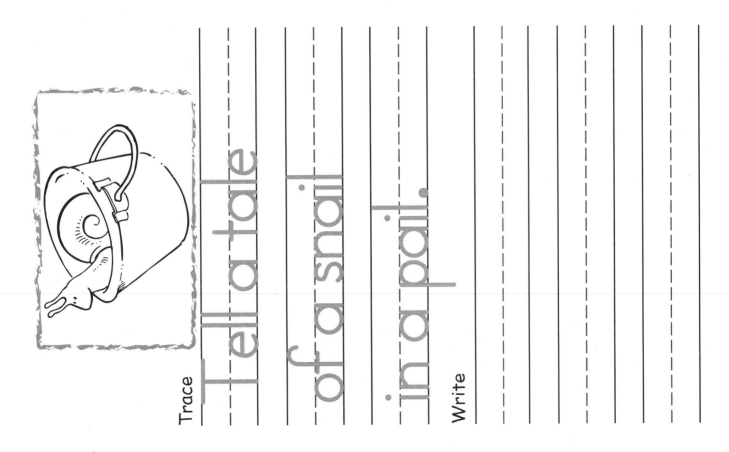

Trace

Tell a tale
of a snail
in a pail.

Write

U u

under

The kitten is under the table.

V v

over

Swing over the river, Fido.

Daily Handwriting Practice • EMC 790

Ww

Ww

Where

Where is Willy the worm?

Xx

Xx

X marks the spot on the map!

The glass holds two cups.
Excellent!

The glass holds two cups.

The pan holds one quart.
Excellent!

The tub holds two wet pups.
Do you have a towel?

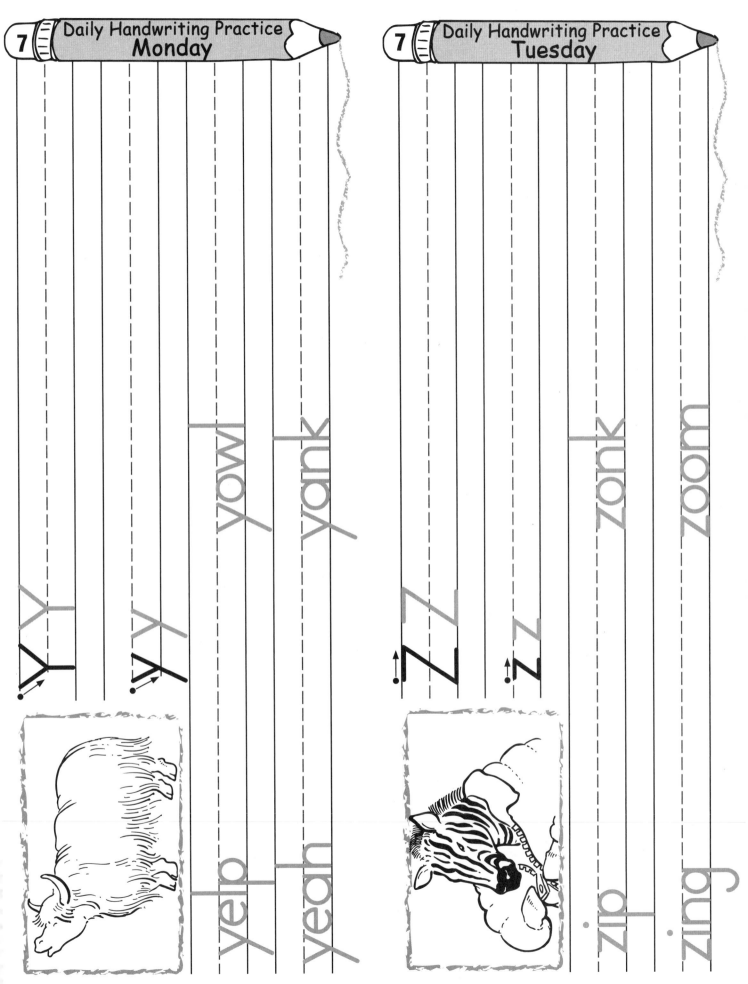

Yy yowl

Yy yank

yelp

yeah

Zz zonk

Zz zoom

zip

zing

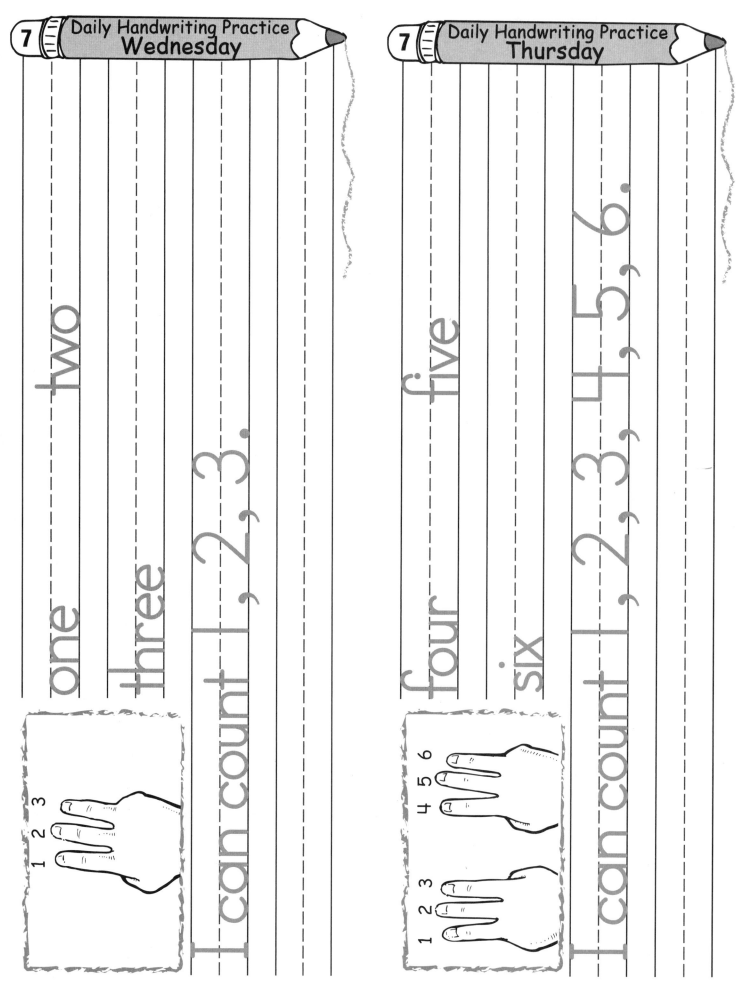

one

two

three

I can count 1, 2, 3.

four

five

six

I can count 1, 2, 3, 4, 5, 6.

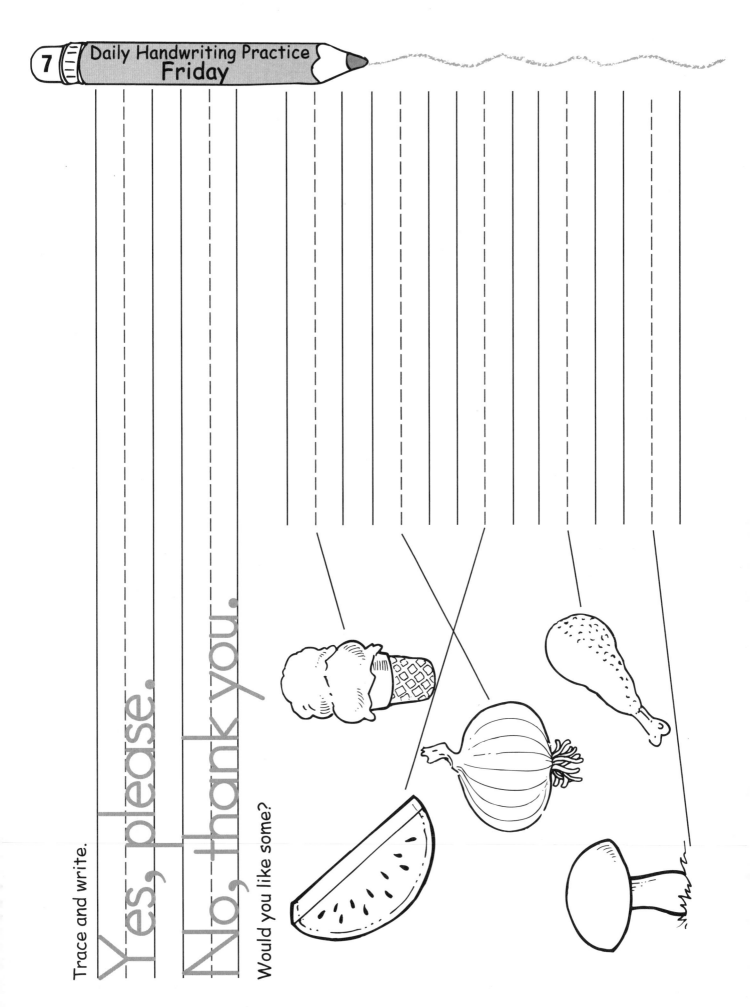

Trace and write.

Yes, please.

No, thank you.

Would you like some?

b

u   e

blue

The blue morpho has two wings.

r   d

e

red

Roses are red, violets are blue.

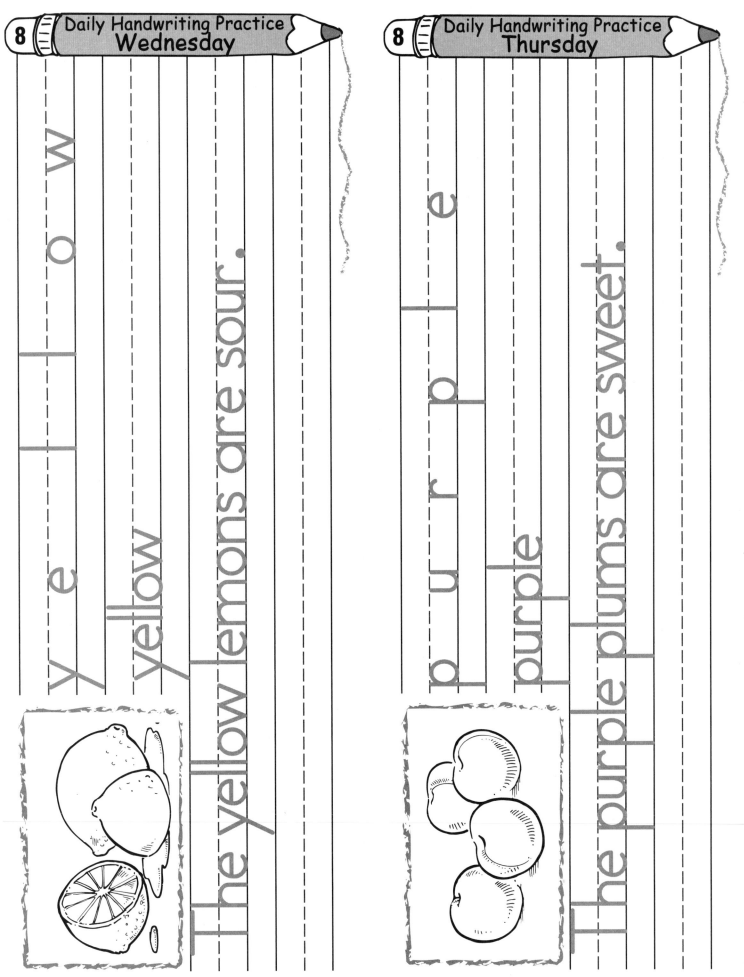

y e l l o w

yellow

The yellow lemons are sour.

p u r p l e

purple

The purple plums are sweet.

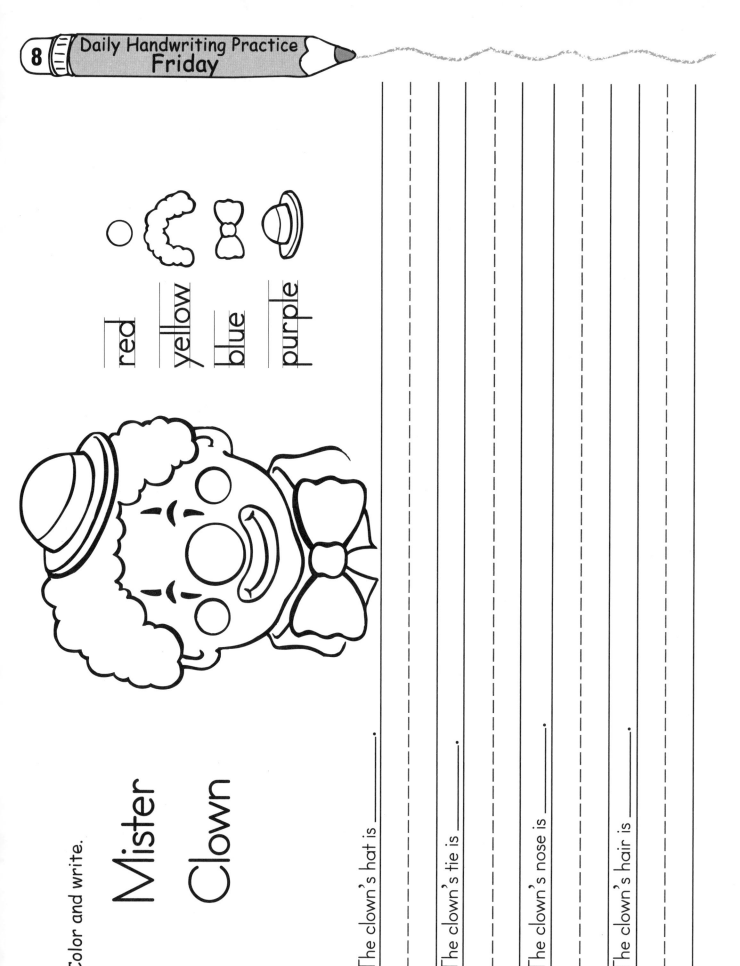

Color and write.

Mister Clown

red
yellow
blue
purple

The clown's hat is _____.

The clown's tie is _____.

The clown's nose is _____.

The clown's hair is _____.

green

g r e e n

green

The green grass tickles my toes.

orange

o r a n g e

orange

I picked an orange pumpkin.

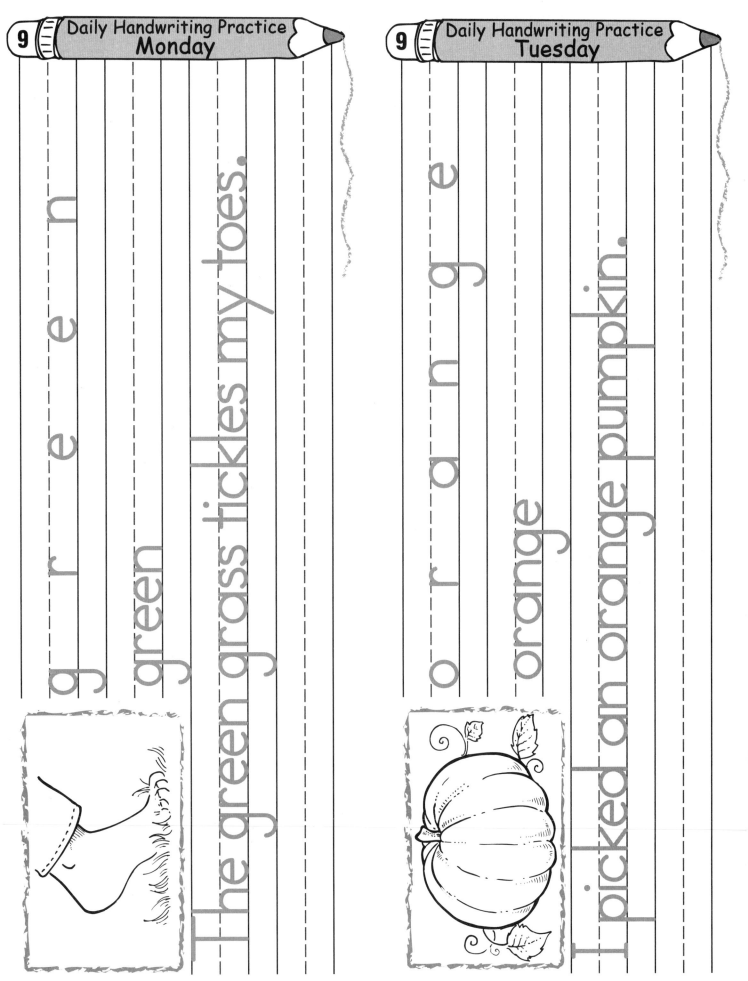

27

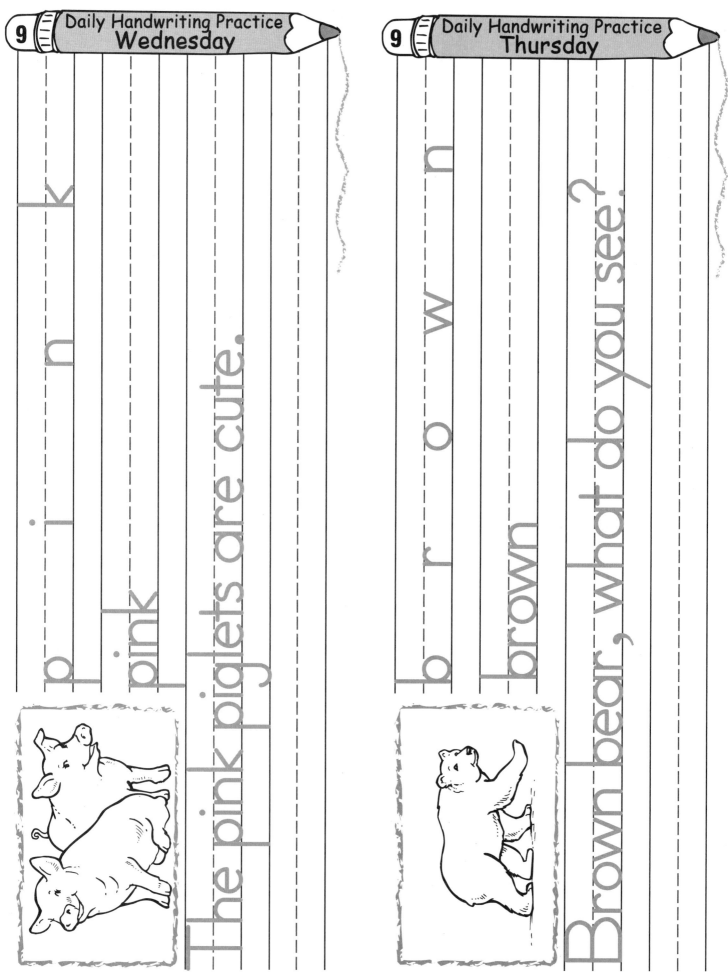

p i n k

pink

The pink piglets are cute.

b r o w n

brown

Brown bear, what do you see?

red
orange
yellow
green
blue
purple

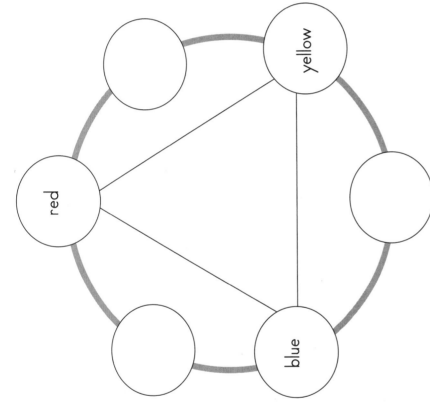

The
Color
Wheel

Color and write.

Red and blue make purple.

Blue and yellow make green.

Yellow and red make orange.

my book

your book

We like to share our books.

his pencil

her pencil

They use their pencils every day.

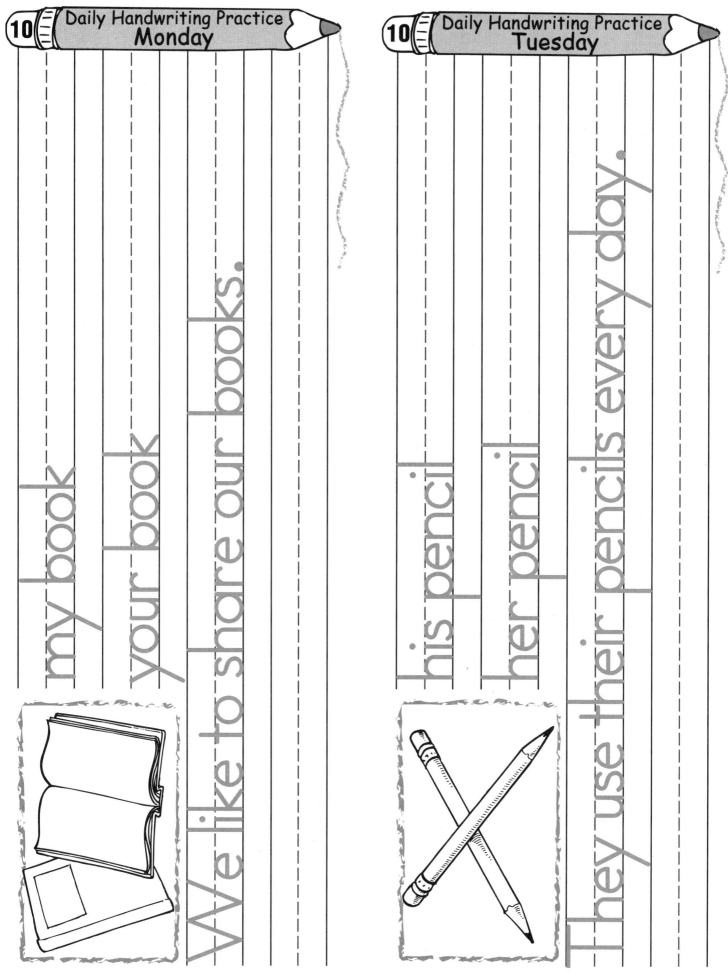

big, sharp scissors

Big, sharp scissors cut paper.

paste

glue

Stick it together with paste or glue.

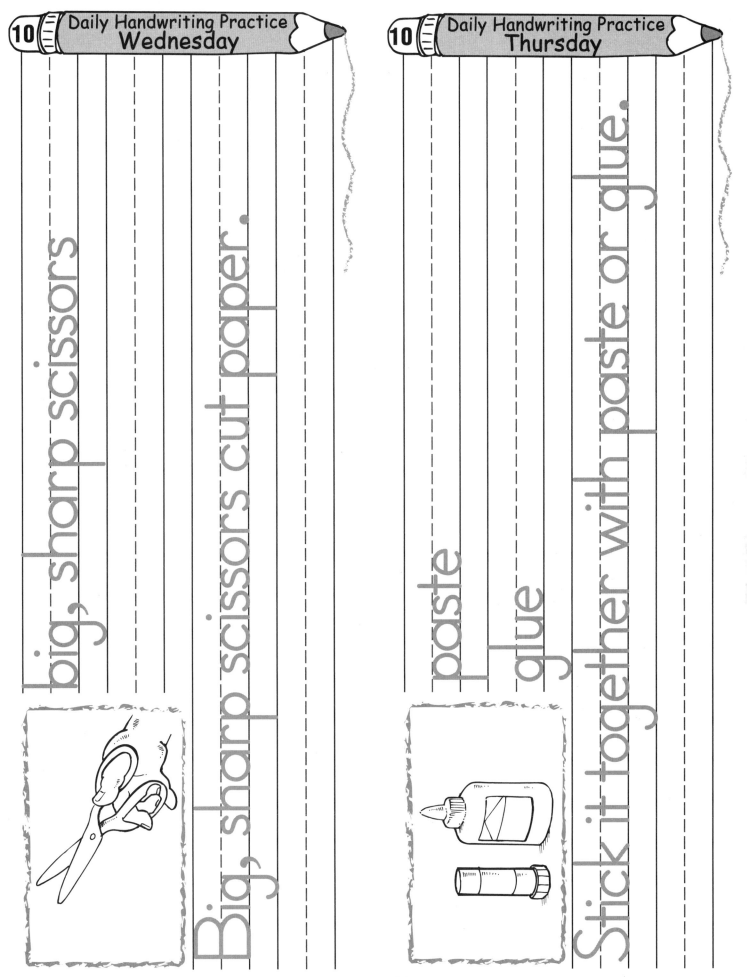

31

At School

We use tools to help us at school.
We use scissors to cut.
We use pencils to write.
We use glue and paste to stick things together.

Copy the story.

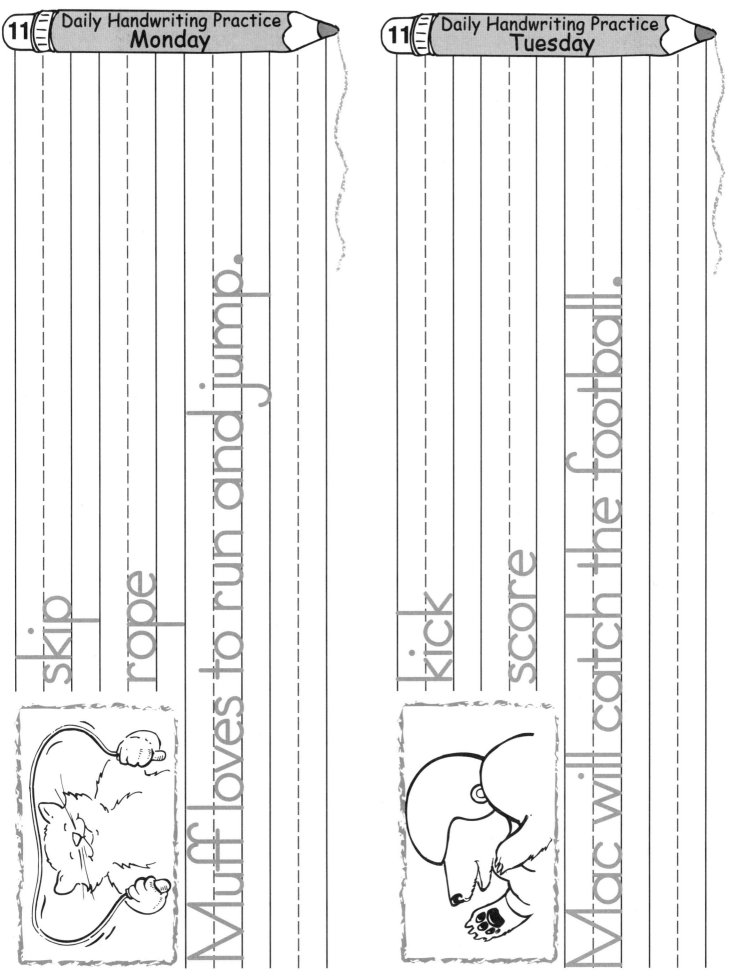

skip

rope

Muff loves to run and jump.

kick

score

Mac will catch the football.

sit up

beg

Did Buster wag his tail?

Good for you.

sing

talk

Can you listen to the parrot?

Shhhhh.

Frogs Hop

We go fast and we go slow.
Watch and see how fast we go.
Run and jump and skip and hop.
We go fast and never stop.

Copy the poem.

35

toast

cereal

I eat a balanced breakfast.

soup

sandwich

I eat a nutritious lunch.

dinner

supper

Come and get it. It's ready.

chips

fruit

I love to eat tasty snacks.

Lettuce Roll-up

Wash one lettuce leaf.
Spread peanut butter on it.
Sprinkle with raisins.
Roll up the leaf.
Eat and enjoy.

Copy the recipe.

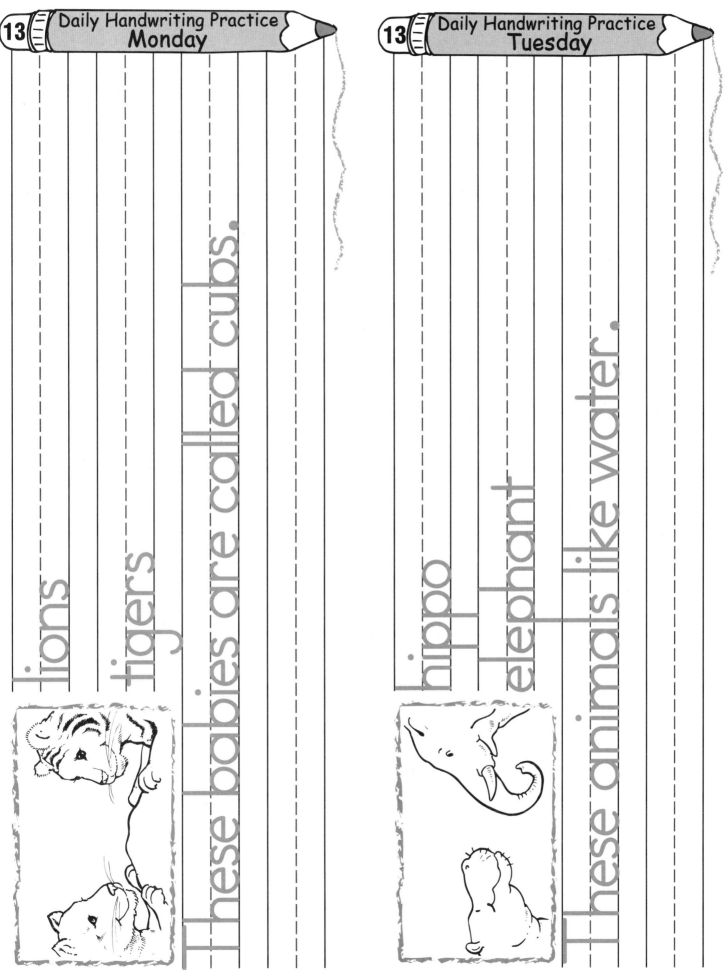

lions

tigers

These babies are called cubs.

hippo

elephant

These animals like water.

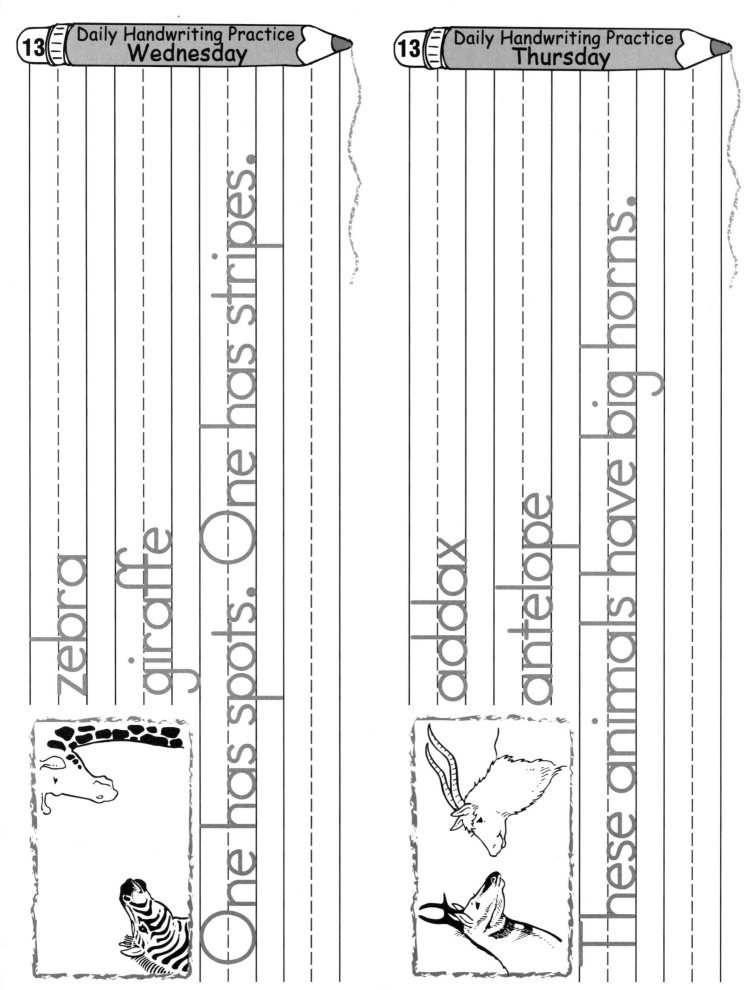

zebra

giraffe

One has spots. One has stripes.

addax

antelope

These animals have big horns.

Name the animal.

Welcome to the Zoo

hippo

elephant

lion

tiger

addax

antelope

giraffe

zebra

41

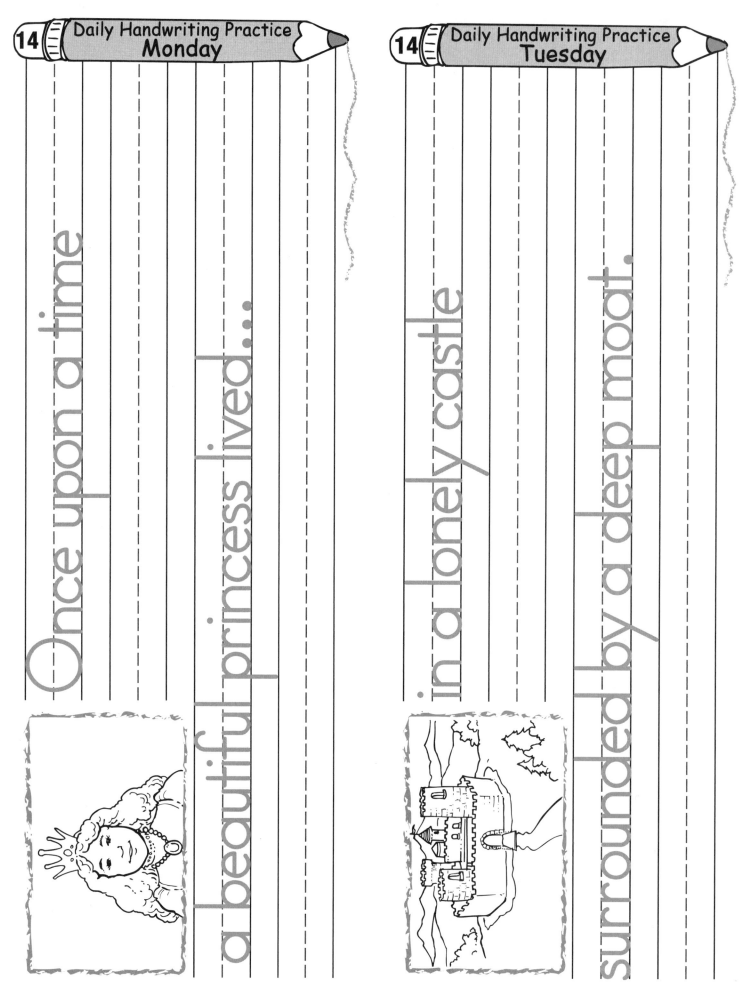

Once upon a time

a beautiful princess lived...

in a lonely castle

surrounded by a deep moat.

42

She sat in the tower

and wished she had a friend.

She was very sad.

Would she ever find a friend?

The Princess

Once upon a time there was a beautiful princess. She lived in a castle with a moat. She had no visitors. She was lonely.

Finish the story.

Word Box

handsome prince

snuggly kitten

happily ever after

Monday

Monday

Monday

Today is marvelous Monday.

Tuesday

Tuesday

Tuesday

Today is terrific Tuesday.

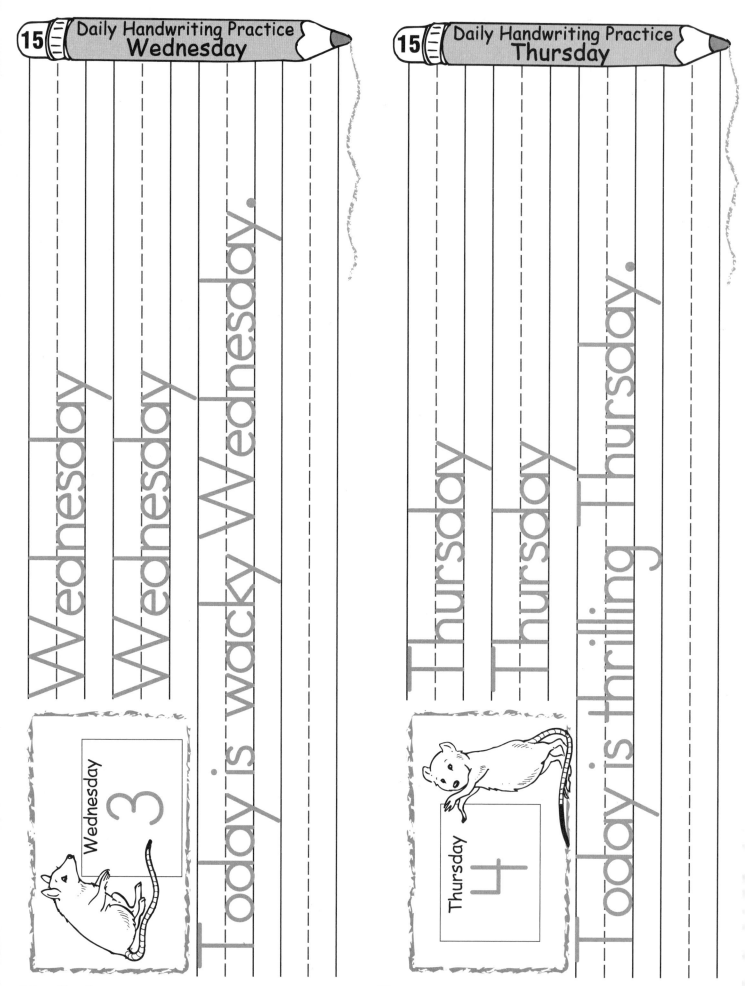

Wednesday

Wednesday

Today is wacky Wednesday.

Wednesday 3

Thursday

Thursday

Today is thrilling Thursday.

Thursday 4

What a Week!

Today is Friday.
Finally, a fun-filled Friday.
We had a marvelous Monday,
a terrific Tuesday,
a wacky Wednesday,
and a thrilling Thursday.

Read and copy.

Today is Friday.

47

What kind of pizza do you like?

veggie

cheese

pepperoni

I like

What kind of sandwich do you like?

ham

tuna

peanut butter

I like

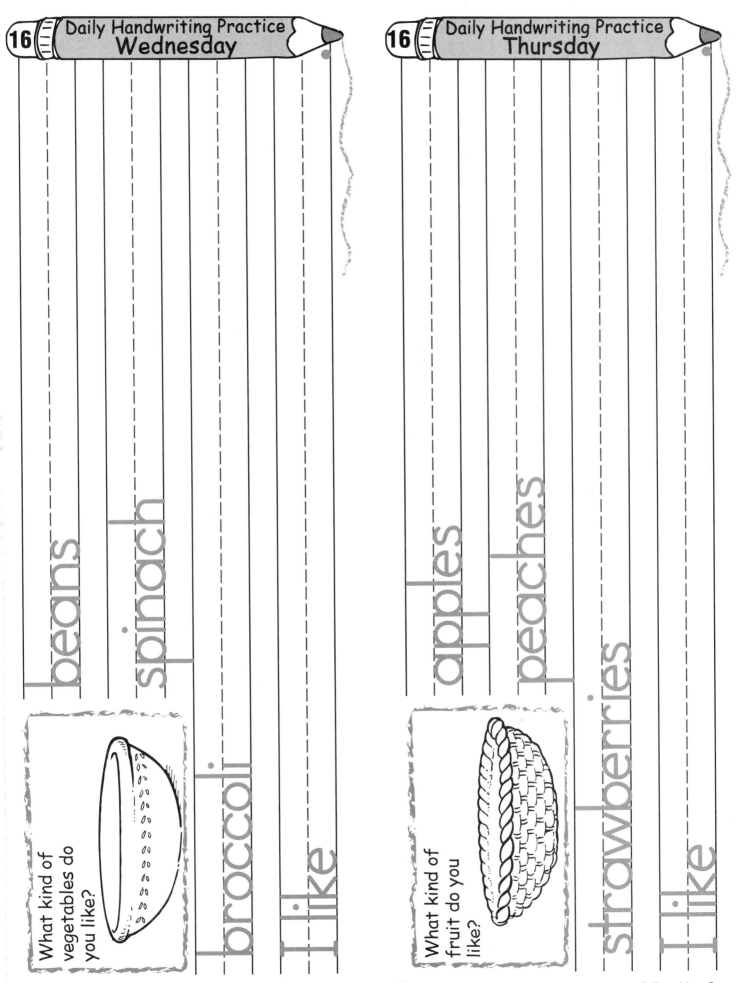

What kind of vegetables do you like?

beans

spinach

broccoli

I like

What kind of fruit do you like?

apples

peaches

strawberries

I like

49

Cooking

Copy this poem.

Measure and pour.
Stir it to mix.
Look at the things
That I can fix.

Pudding, pretzels
Sandwiches, too.
I think it's fun
To cook for you.

Daily Handwriting Practice • EMC 790

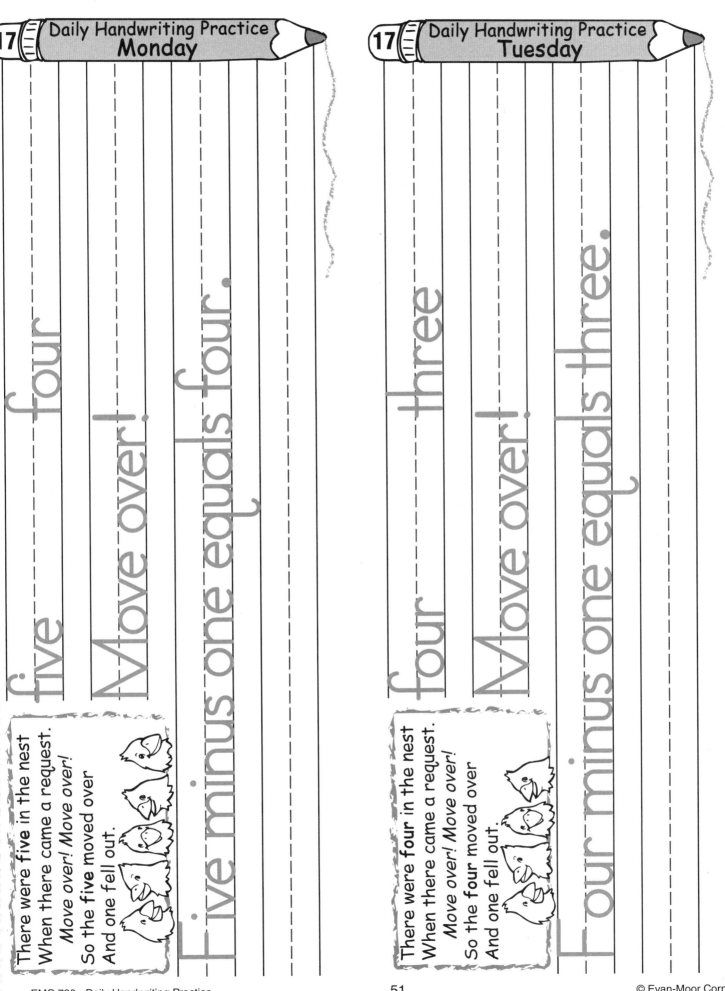

five   four

Move over!

Five minus one equals four.

There were **five** in the nest
When there came a request.
Move over! Move over!
So the **five** moved over
And one fell out.

four   three

Move over!

Four minus one equals three.

There were **four** in the nest
When there came a request.
Move over! Move over!
So the **four** moved over
And one fell out.

51

three

two

Move over!

Three minus one equals two.

There were **three** in the nest
When there came a request.
Move over! Move over!
So the **three** moved over
And one fell out.

two

one

Move over!

Two minus one equals one.

There were **two** in the nest
When there came a request.
Move over! Move over!
So the **two** moved over
And one fell out.

There was **one** in the nest
And, at last, no request.
Just a quiet time for rest.
Shhhhhh.

Trace and write the numbers.

five

four

three

two

one

Sweet dreams.

Sleep tight.

53

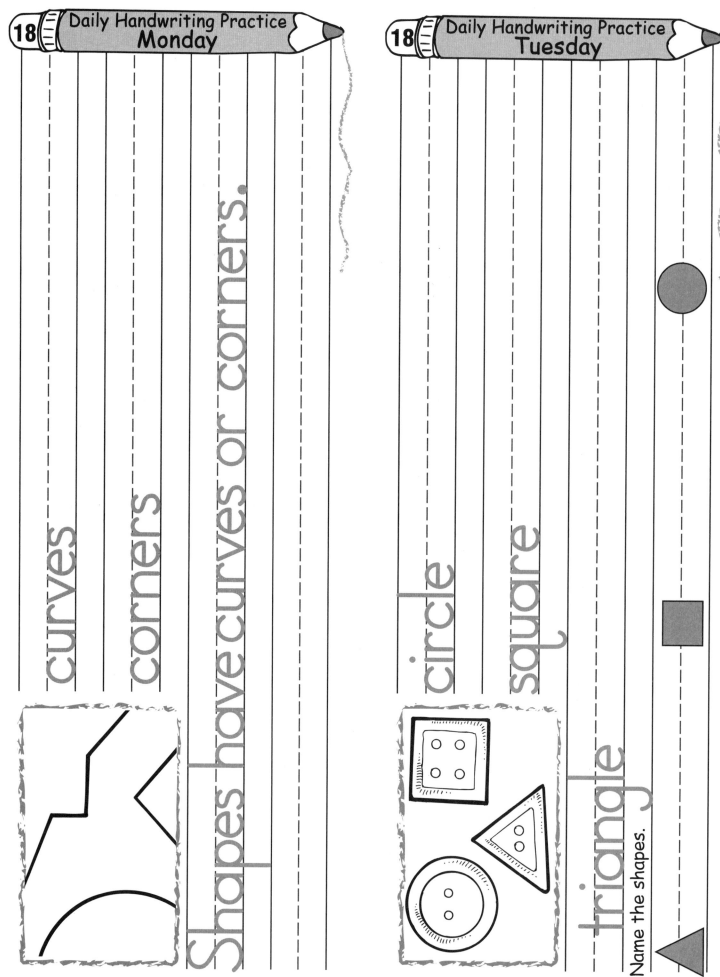

curves

corners

Shapes have curves or corners.

circle

square

triangle

Name the shapes.

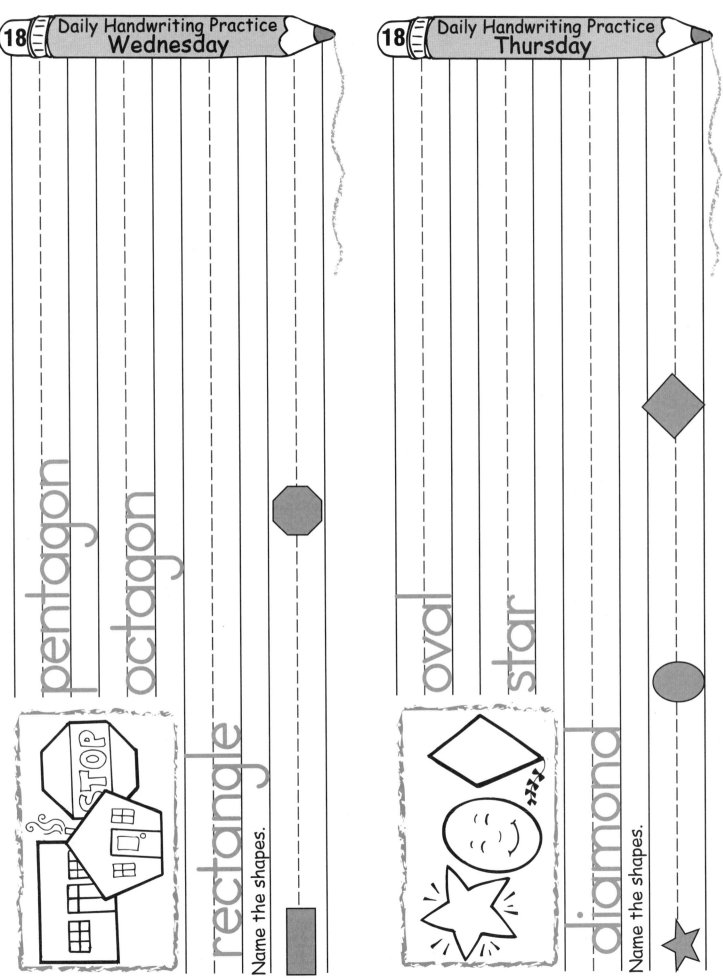

pentagon

octagon

rectangle

Name the shapes.

oval

star

diamond

Name the shapes.

Trace and finish the picture.

Draw a square head.

Add a rectangle body.

Make two arms and legs.

Draw a funny face on it.

Draw a triangle for a hat.

Copy the directions.

What did you make?

penny

nickel

How can you make ten cents?

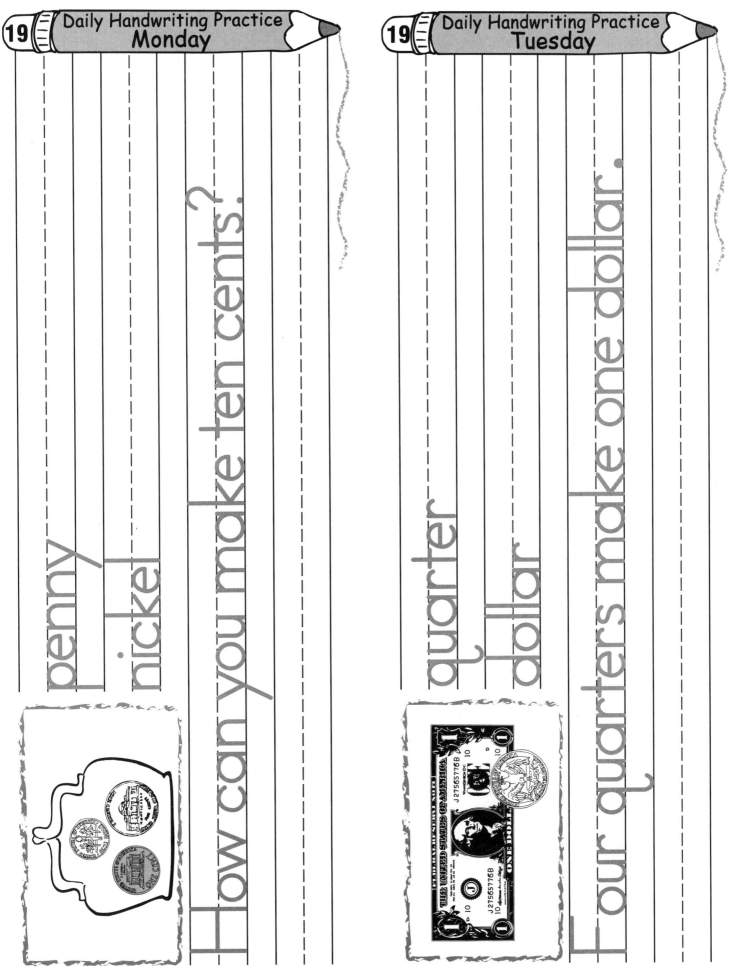

quarter

dollar

our quarters make one dollar.

57

dollar

bills

I carry my dollar bills in a wallet.

coins

change

Put your coins in the bank.

Money

Mom keeps her money in a purse.

Dad keeps his money in his pocket.

Granny keeps her money in a pouch.

Buster keeps his money in a bank.

Copy the sentences.

Where do you keep your money?

first

second

I do won first place at the fair.

third

fourth

The gray ant is in third place.

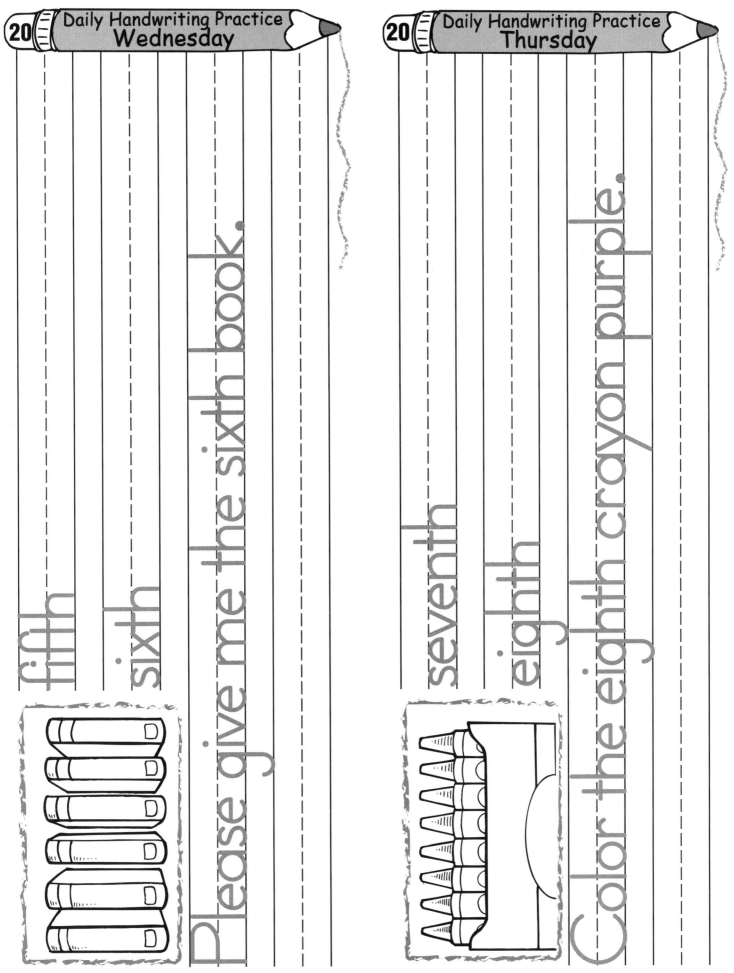

fifth

sixth

Please give me the sixth book.

seventh

eighth

Color the eighth crayon purple.

61

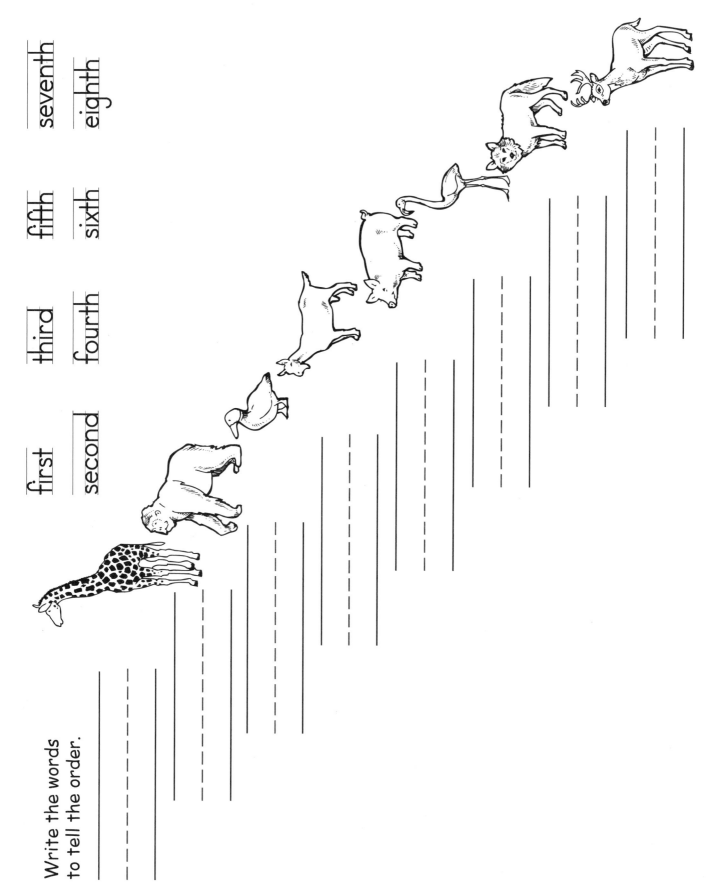

first   second   third   fourth   fifth   sixth   seventh   eighth

Write the words
to tell the order.

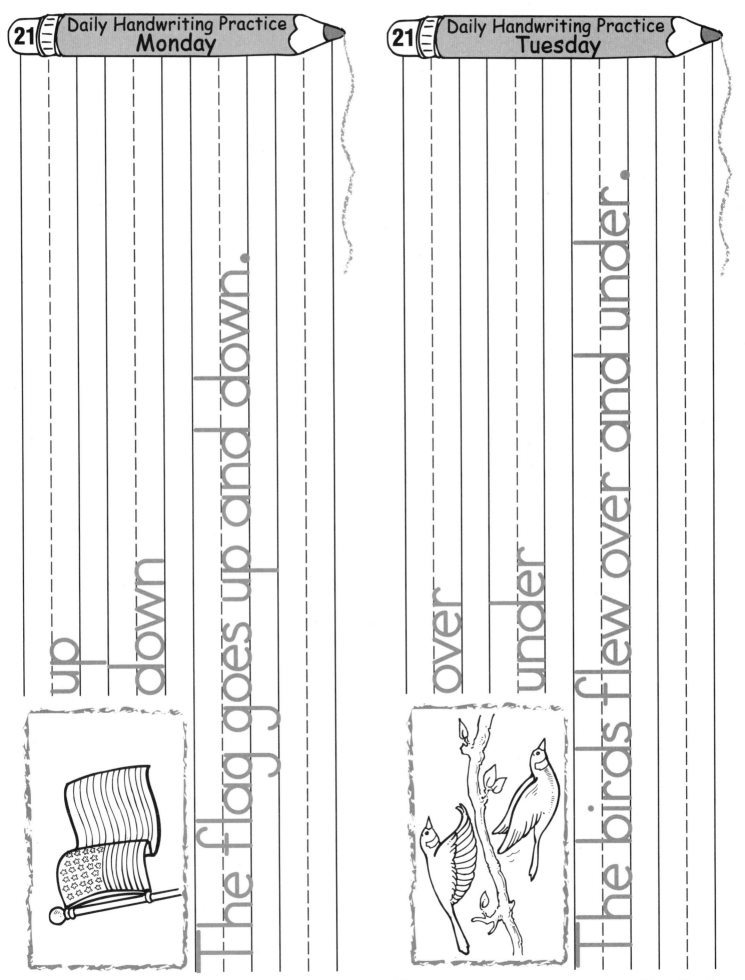

up

down

The flag goes up and down.

over

under

The birds flew over and under.

behind

in front

The goat is behind the gate.

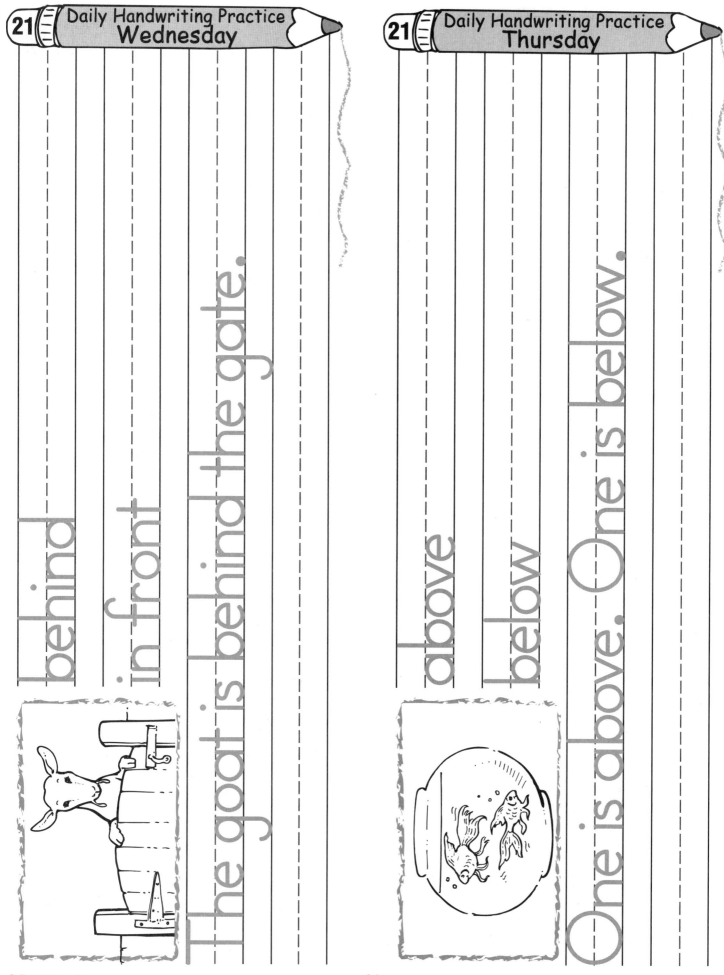

above

below

One is above. One is below.

Singing in the Rain

Match the opposites.

up   behind

in front of   under

over   below

above   down

Copy the sentences to tell about the picture.

The bird is above the mushroom.

- -

The mouse is below the mushroom.

- -

The fence is behind the mushroom.

- -

The leaf is in front of the mushroom.

- -

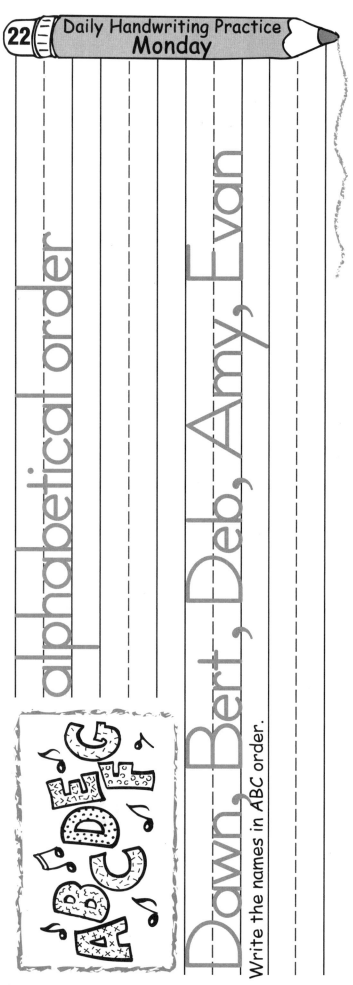

alphabetical order

Dawn, Bert, Deb, Amy, Evan

Write the names in *ABC* order.

I know ABC order.

Joe, Hank, Kent, Lian, Fran

Write the names in *ABC* order.

I use ABC order.

Rosa, Peg, Olaf, Said, Quon

Write the names in ABC order.

At the end is x, y, z.

Zach, Tila, Will, Vicki, Uri

Write the names in ABC order.

67

Write the letters of the alphabet.

Aa

Nn

Cc

Ww

mothers

fathers

Moms and dads are parents.

grandparents

We love our grandparents.

Grandma Grandpa

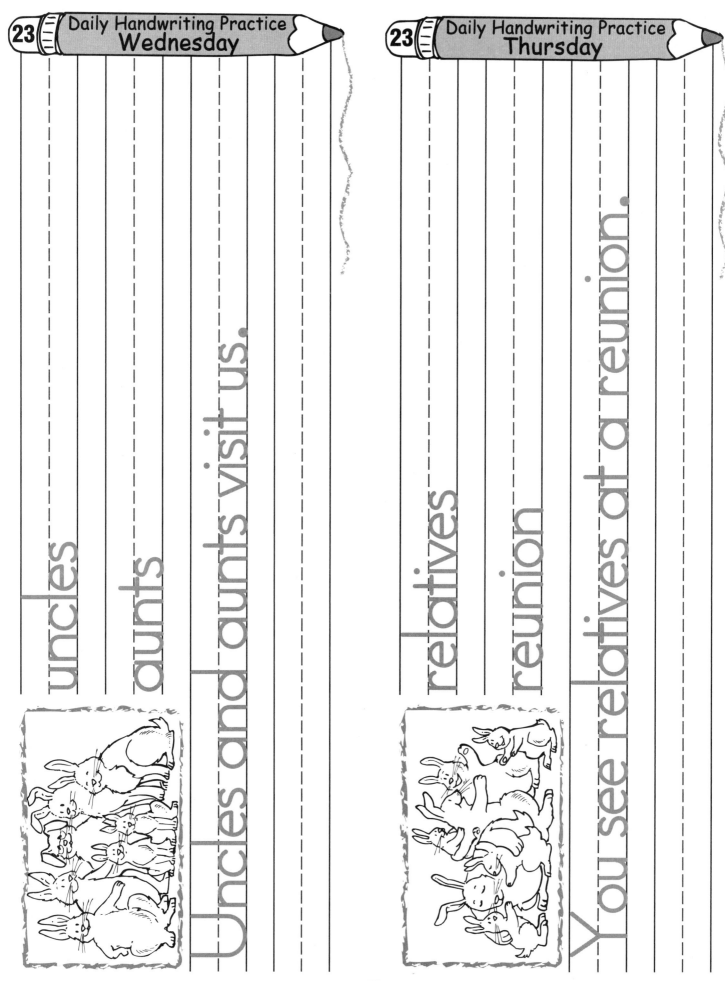

uncles

aunts

Uncles and aunts visit us.

relatives

reunion

You see relatives at a reunion.

Copy the poem.

The Family Reunion

Happy smiles,
Lots of names,
Yummy food,
Crazy games,
Hugs and kisses,
Teary eyes,
Handshakes, backslaps,
Warm good-byes.

71

our solar system

eight planets and one sun

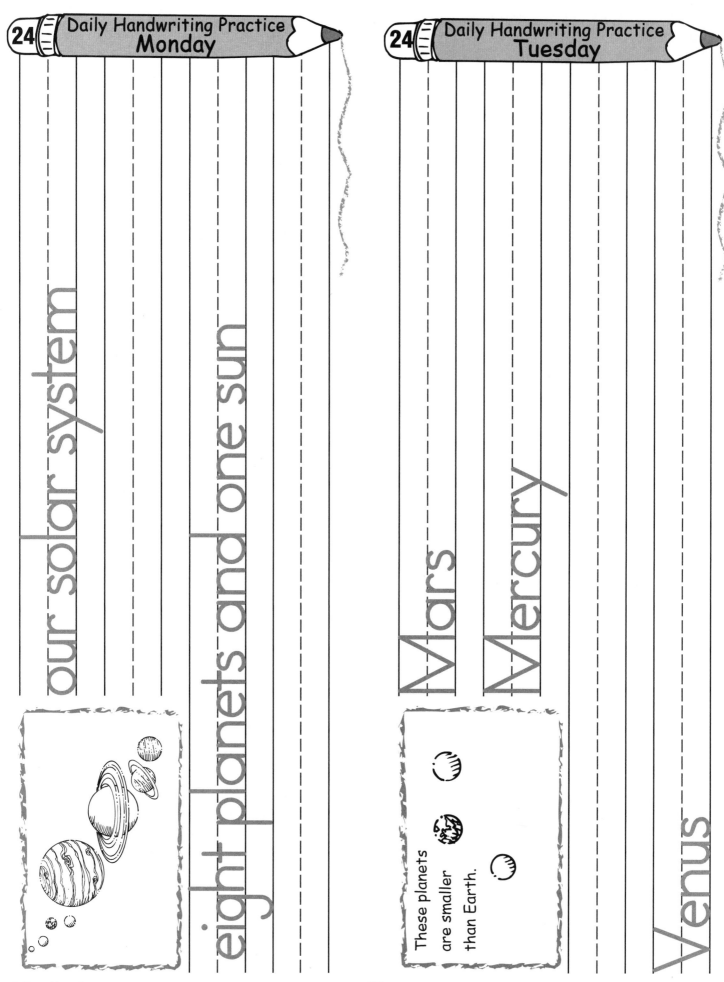

Mars

Mercury

Venus

These planets are smaller than Earth.

72

Neptune

Saturn

Name planets bigger than Earth:

asteroids

comets

Look for them in a telescope.

Our Solar System

Write the names of the planets.

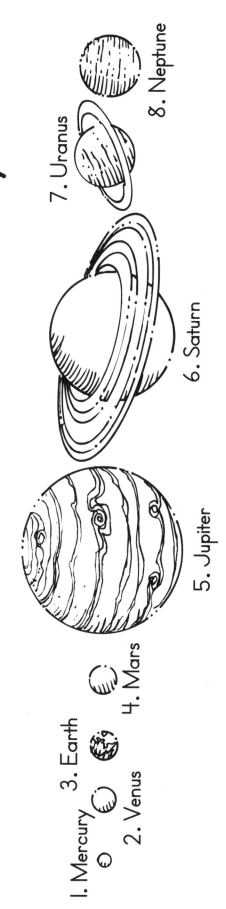

1. Mercury
2. Venus
3. Earth
4. Mars
5. Jupiter

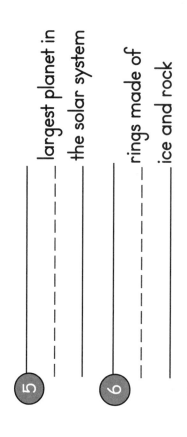

6. Saturn

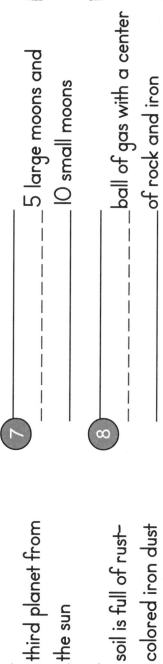

7. Uranus
8. Neptune

5 ○ largest planet in ----- the solar system

6 ○ rings made of ----- ice and rock

7 ○ 5 large moons and ----- 10 small moons

8 ○ ball of gas with a center ----- of rock and iron

1 ○ a small, ----- rocky planet

2 ○ covered in thick, ----- yellow clouds

3 ○ third planet from ----- the sun

4 ○ soil is full of rust- ----- colored iron dust

74

January

February

March

There are
12 months
every year.
See how well I write
them here.

The first three
months are:

April

May

June

There are
12 months
every year.
See how well I write
them here.

The next three
months are:

July
August
September

October
November
December

There are
12 months
every year.
See how well I write
them here.

The next three
months are:

There are
12 months
every year.
See how well I write
them here.

The last three
months are:

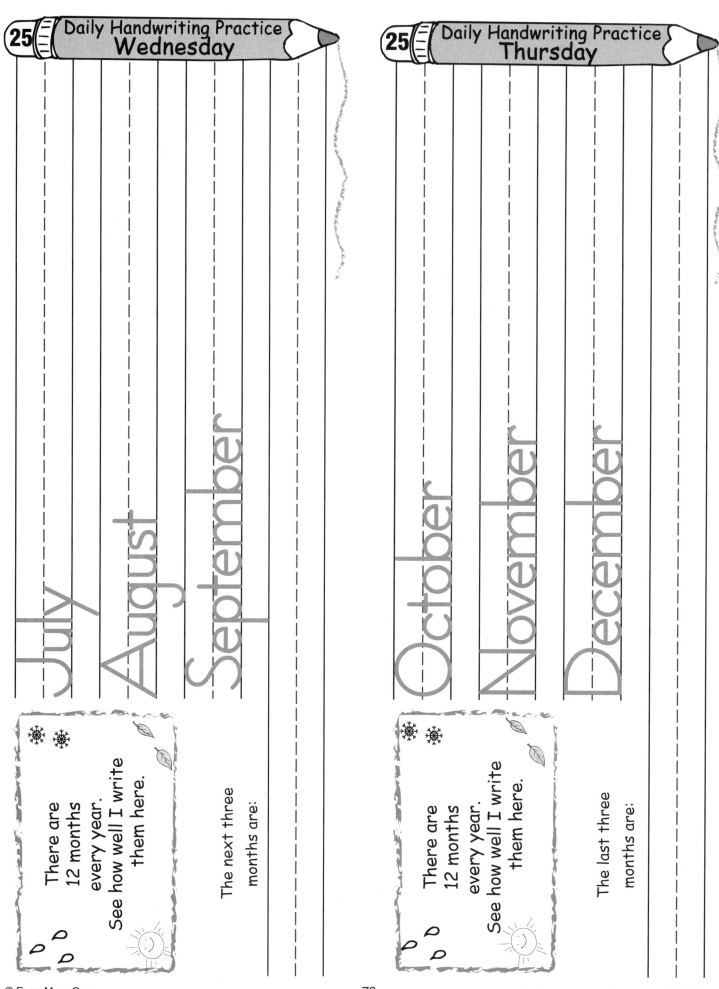

May	January	August
December	July	November
June	October	February
April	September	March

The Calendar

Write the names of the months in order.

Save the Earth.

It is our job to use resources wisely.

Help reduce waste.

Help reduce trash and garbage.

Reuse things at home.

Turn your trash into treasures.

Recycle your trash.

Remake the old into new things.

Save the Earth

Make a plan for helping to protect our environment.
Write what you will do. Use your best handwriting.

I will reduce.

I will reuse.

I will recycle.

I will

continents

There are seven continents.

North

South

America

Write the names of the continents here.

1

2

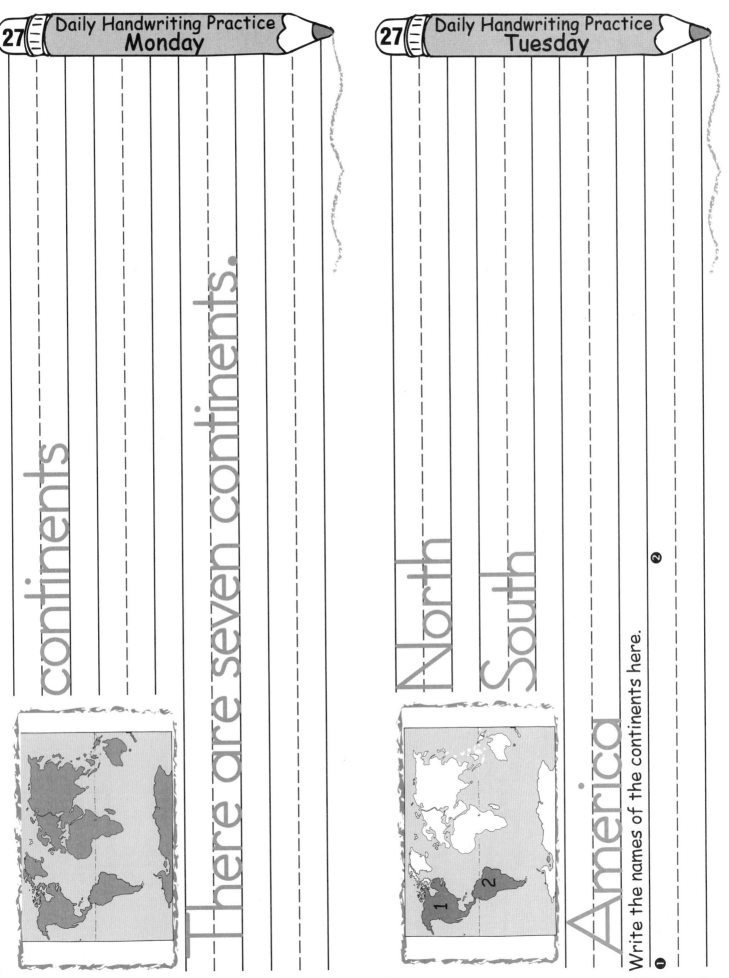

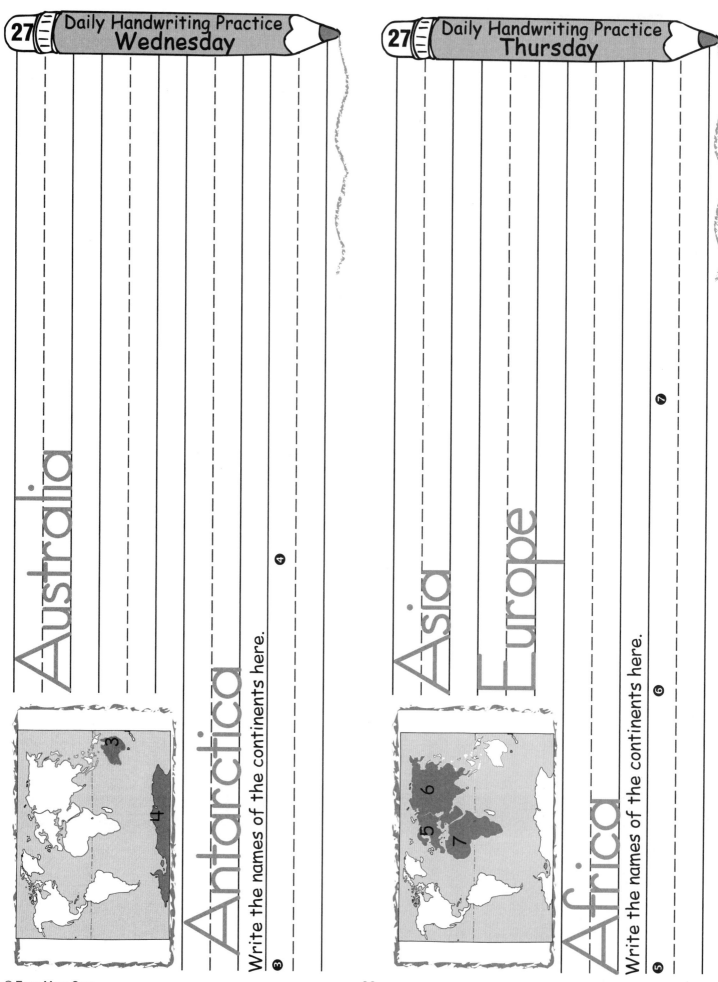

Australia

Antarctica

Write the names of the continents here.

❸

❹

Asia

Europe

Africa

Write the names of the continents here.

❺

❻

❼

1. _____
2. _____
3. _____
4. _____
5. _____
6. _____
7. _____

Label the continents.

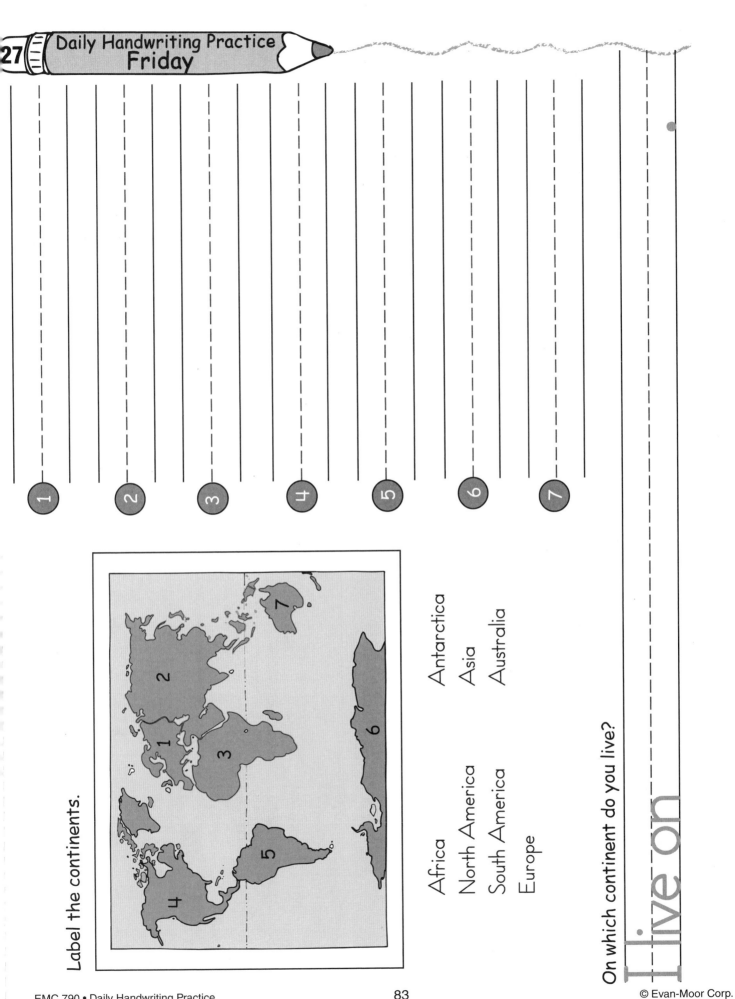

Africa
North America
South America
Europe

Antarctica
Asia
Australia

On which continent do you live?

I live on _____

The outside layer of the Earth is called the crust.

crust

rock

soil

Rock and soil form the crust.

The mantle is made of rock and metal.

mantle

mantle

metal

The mantle is below the crust.

core

under

Under the mantle is the core.

The core is under the mantle.

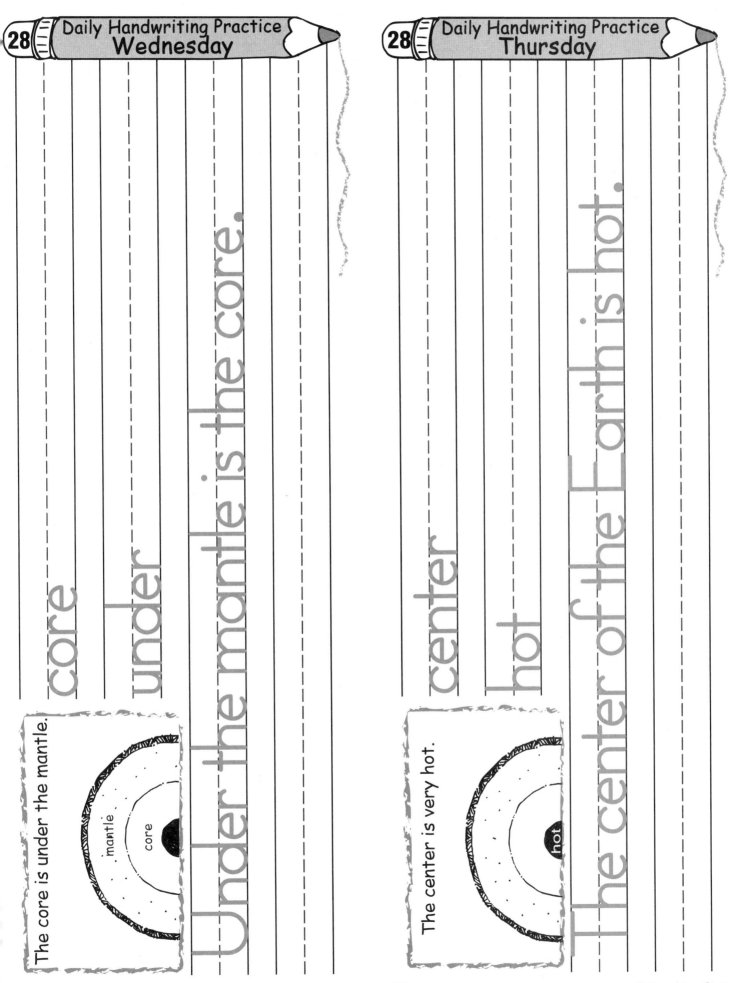

mantle

core

center

hot

The center of the Earth is hot.

The center is very hot.

hot

85

Earth's Layers

Label the Earth's layers.

1
2
3
4

We walk on the Earth's

crust   core   mantle   center

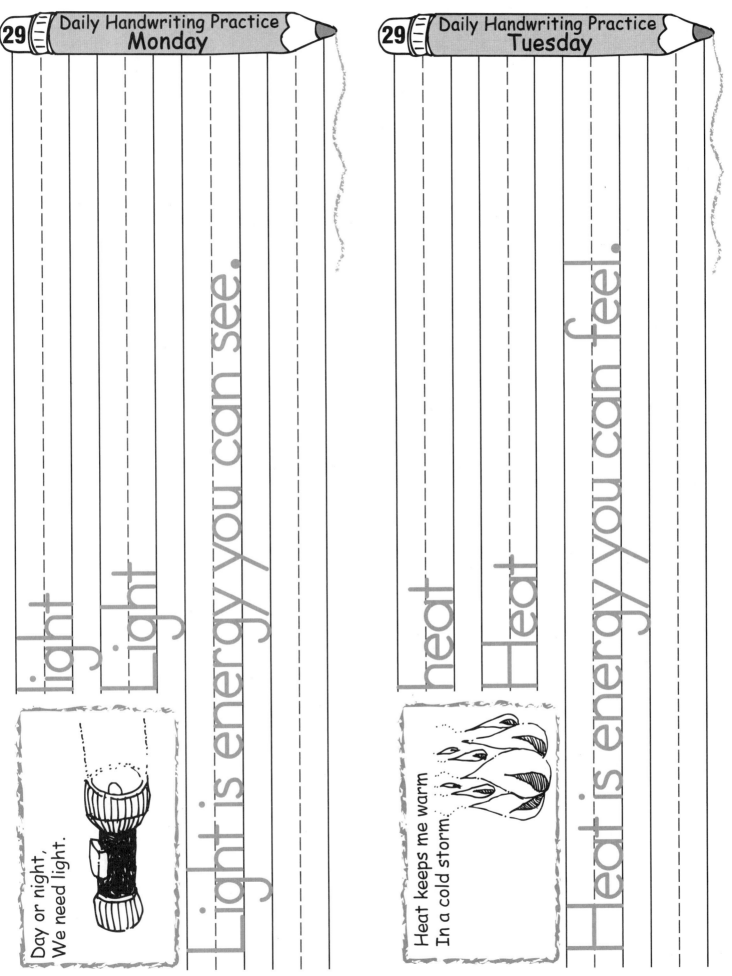

Monday

light

Light

Day or night,
We need light.

Light is energy you can see.

Tuesday

heat

Heat

Heat keeps me warm
In a cold storm.

Heat is energy you can feel.

sound

Sound

Sound is energy you can hear.

Just use your ear.
It's loud and clear.

energy

Energy

Energy has different forms.

Light, heat,
and sound
are all forms
of energy.

88

Energy Is All Around Us

Energy is all around us.

The light you see is energy.

The sound you hear is energy.

The heat you feel is energy.

Energy is all around us.

Copy the information.

Fractions have to be equal pieces.

fraction

fractions

A fraction is part of a whole.

When something is divided into two equal pieces, the pieces are called **halves**.

one-half

two halves

The cupcake is divided into halves.

When something is divided into three equal pieces, we call the pieces **thirds**.

third

thirds

The pie is divided into thirds.

When something is divided into four equal pieces, we call the pieces **fourths**.

fourth

fourths

The pizza is divided into fourths.

Fractions

three-fourths

two-thirds

one-third

Write how much is shaded.

one-fourth

one-half

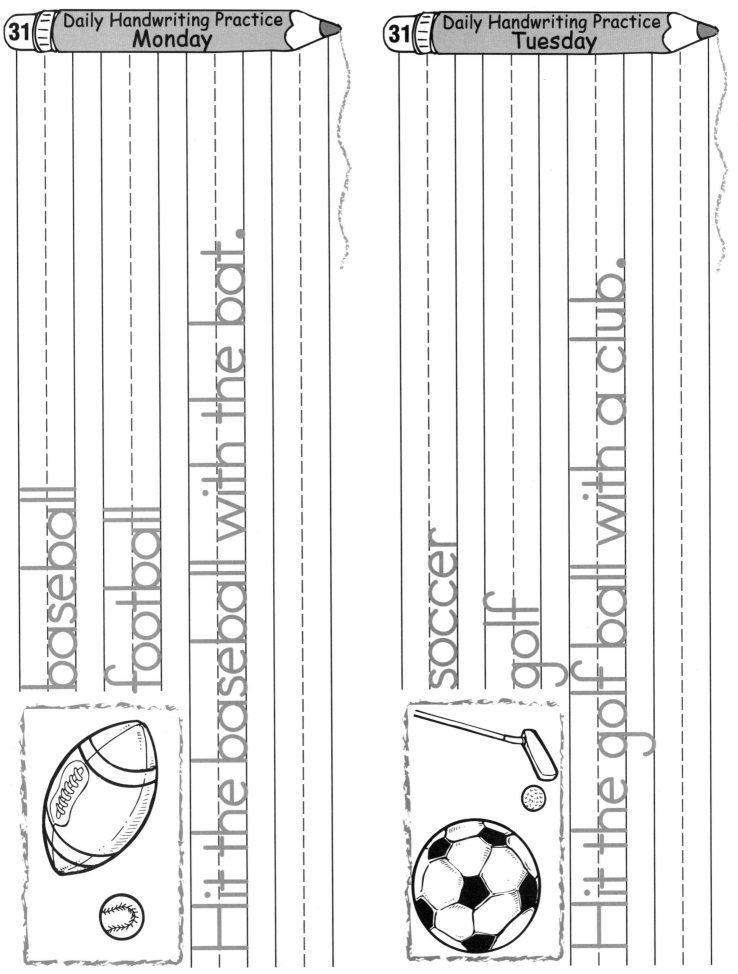

baseball

football

Hit the baseball with the bat.

soccer

golf

Hit the golf ball with a club.

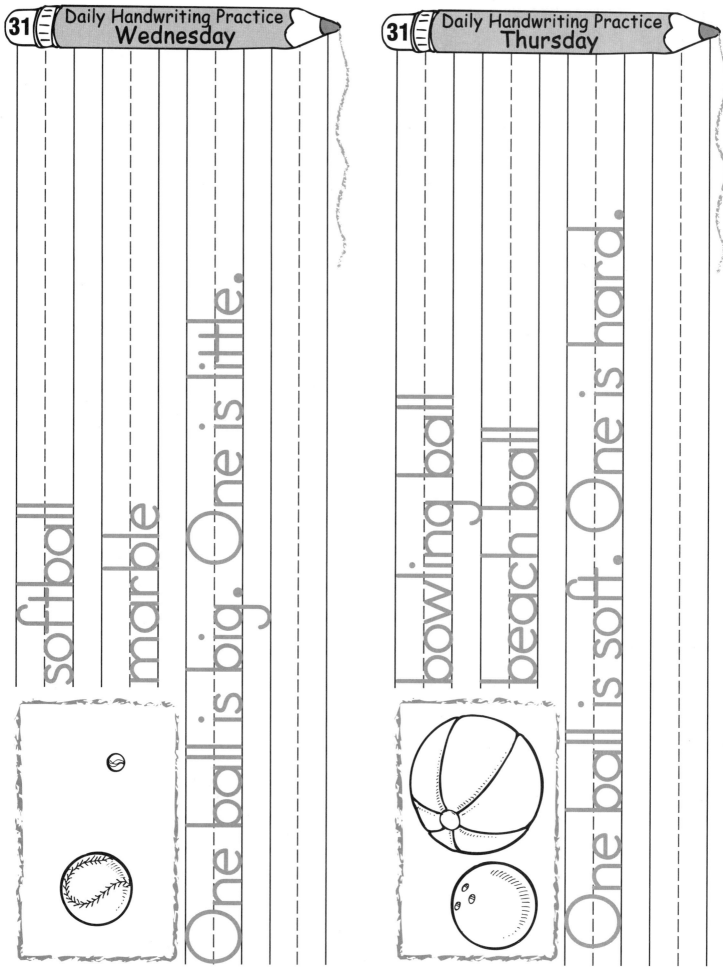

softball

marble

One ball is big. One is little.

bowling ball

beach ball

One ball is soft. One is hard.

Copy the poem.

Let's Play Ball!

Hit them. Catch them.
Throw them back.
Hike them to the
Quarterback.

Kick them. Roll them.
Blow them up.
Putt them into the
Little cup.

roll

flatten

I can flatten my clay.

Roll out the clay.
It's time to play.

I can flatten my clay.

coil

fold

I can shape my clay into a pot.

Make a long snake
Or a pat-a-cake.

I can shape my clay into a pot.

bake

fire

I can bake my clay in the sun.

Bake your project
in the sun
Or in an oven when
you're done.

paint

glaze

I can brush paint on my clay.

Brush on the shine.
It looks mighty fine.

Baker's Clay

What You Need

- bowl
- spoon
- 4 scoops of flour
- 1 scoop of salt
- $1\frac{1}{2}$ scoops of warm water

What You Do

1. Dissolve the salt in warm water.
2. Stir as you add the flour.
3. Knead the dough for 5 minutes.
4. Put the dough into a plastic bag.

Copy the steps here that tell what to do.

1.

2.

3.

4.

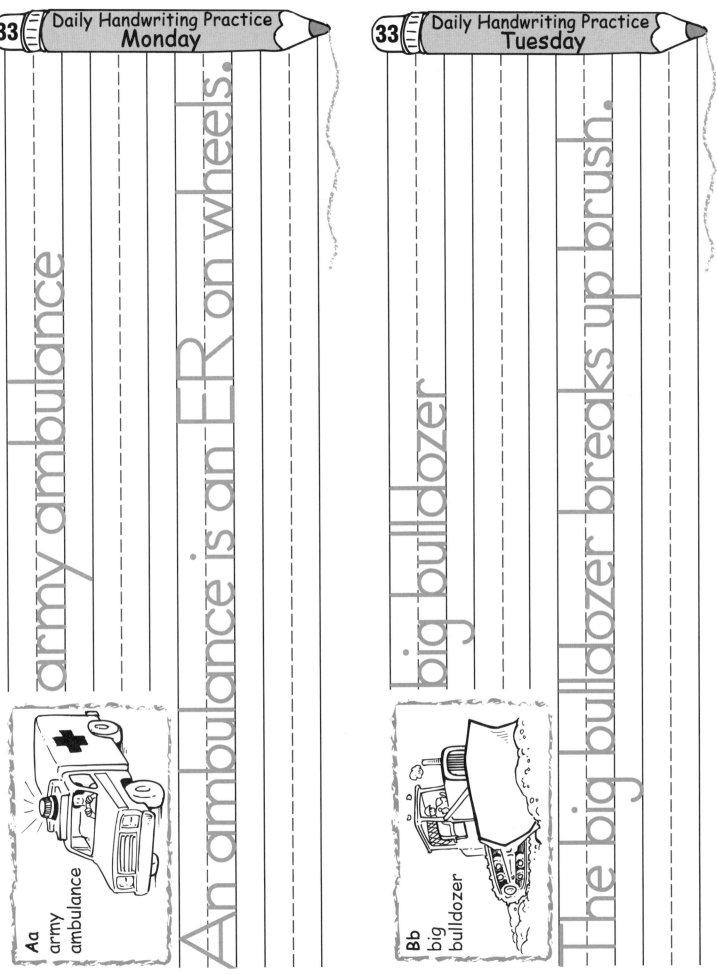

army ambulance

An ambulance is an ER on wheels.

Aa
army
ambulance

big bulldozer

The big bulldozer breaks up brush.

Bb
big
bulldozer

99

Cc
cozy
carriage

cozy carriage

Caution:
Be careful with
your carriage.

The carriage coasts down the hill.

Dd
dusty
dump truck

dusty dump truck

The dump truck delivers dirt.

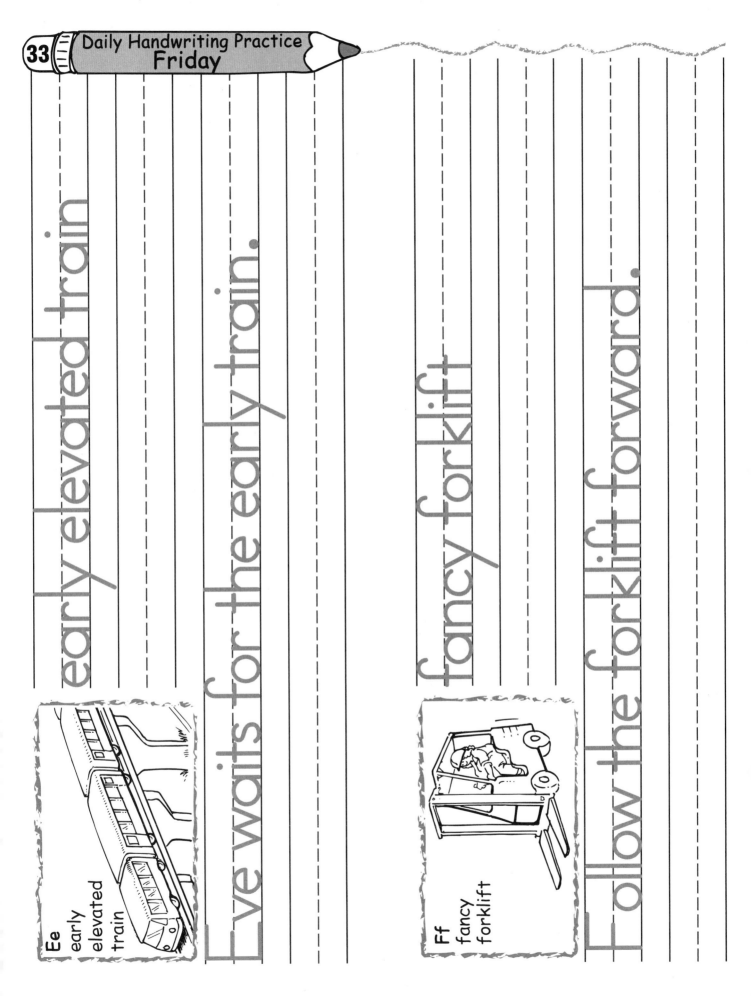

early elevated train.

Eve waits for the early train.

Ee
early
elevated
train

fancy forklift

Follow the forklift forward.

Ff
fancy
forklift

gas-gulping go-cart

Go get some gas for the go-cart.

Gg
gas-gulping
go-cart

high-flying helicopter

The helicopter hovers nearby.

Hh
high-flying
helicopter

important icebreaker

The icebreaker plows through.

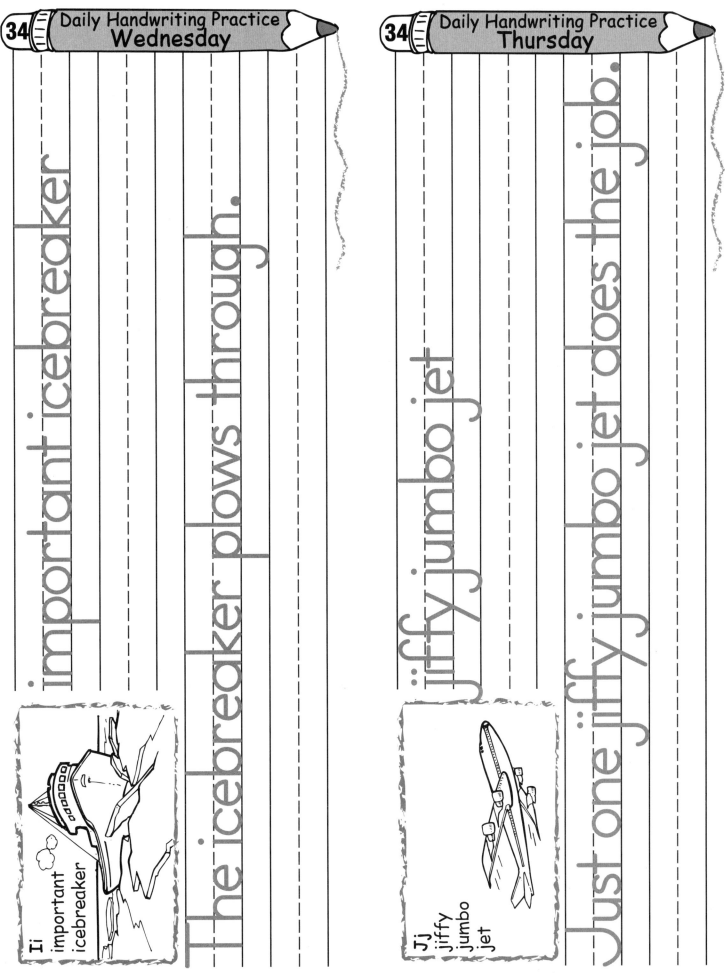

Ii important icebreaker

jiffy jumbo jet

Just one jiffy jumbo jet does the job.

Jj jiffy jumbo jet

keen kayak

A kayak is a kind of canoe.

Kk
keen
kayak

long limousine

The long limousine led the line.

Ll
long
limousine

Daily Handwriting Practice • EMC 790

Mom's motorcycle

Mom's motorcycle moved quickly.

Mm
Mom's
motorcycle

new nuclear sub

The nuclear sub navigated slowly.

Nn
new
nuclear sub

105

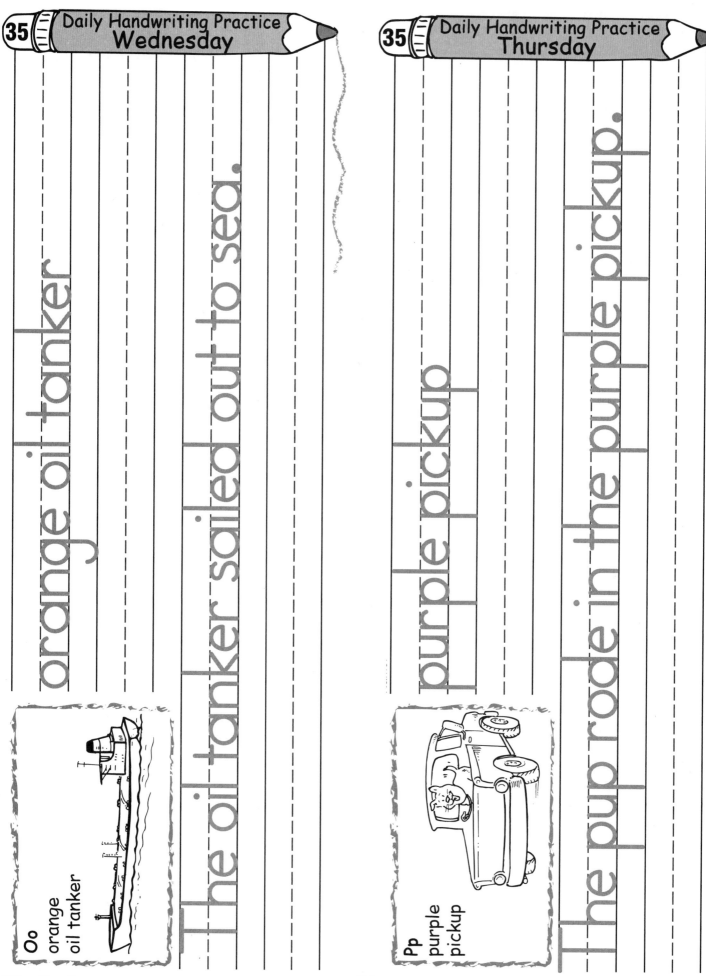

orange oil tanker

The oil tanker sailed out to sea.

Oo
orange
oil tanker

purple pickup

The pup rode in the purple pickup.

Pp
purple
pickup

quiet QE II

Qq
quiet
QE II

The QE II is an ocean liner.

racing roadster

Rr
racing
roadster

The roadster roared up the road.

107

strong steamroller

The steamroller squashed the dirt.

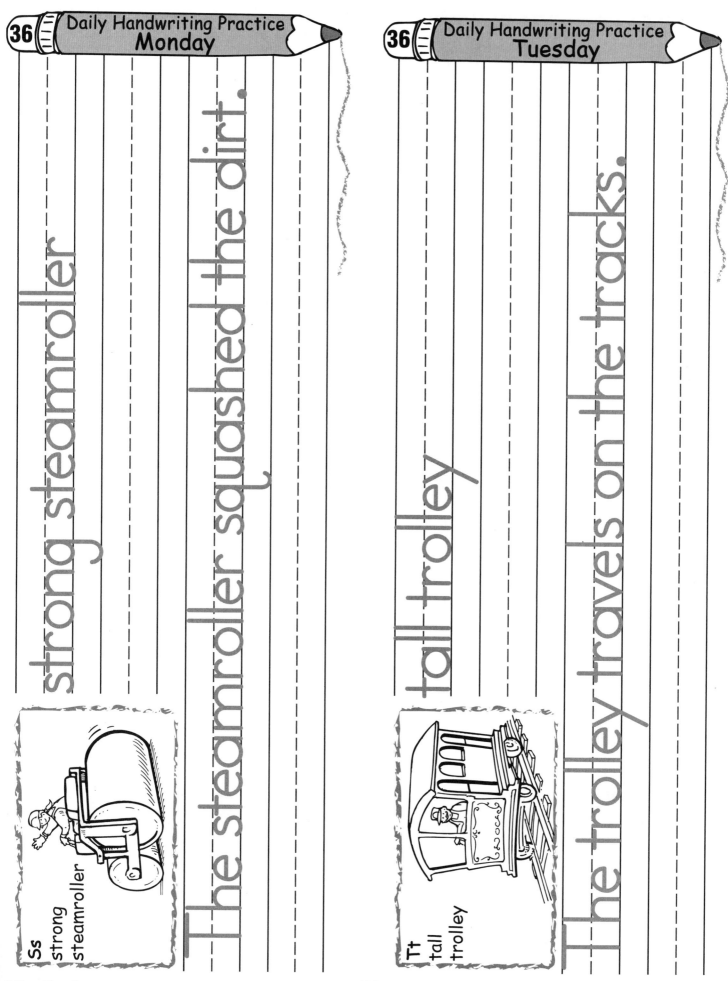

Ss
strong
steamroller

tall trolley

The trolley travels on the tracks.

Tt
tall
trolley

useful unicycle

The unicycle was unusual.

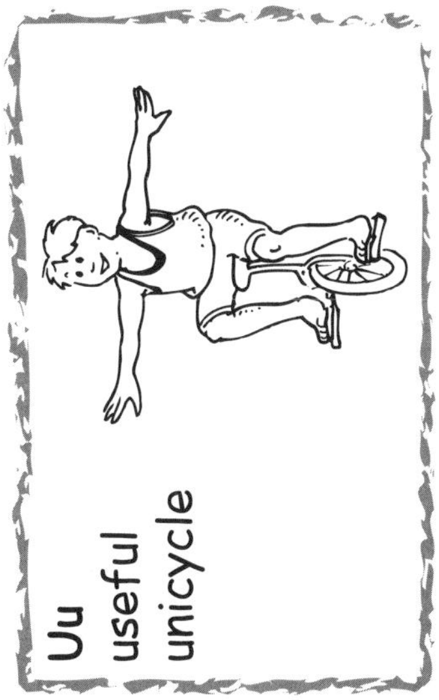

Uu
useful
unicycle

various vessels

Vessels transport passengers.

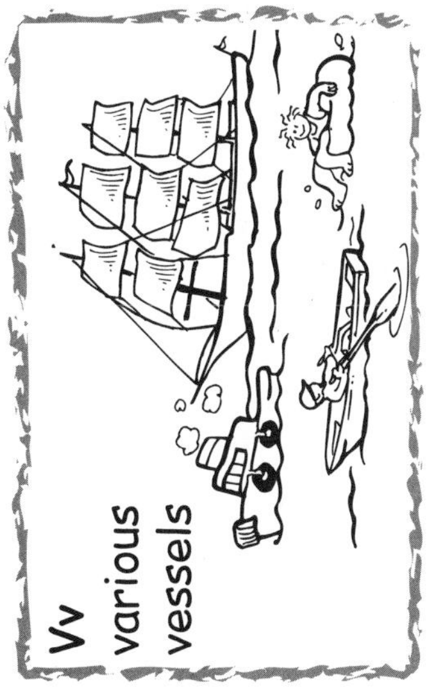

Vv
various
vessels

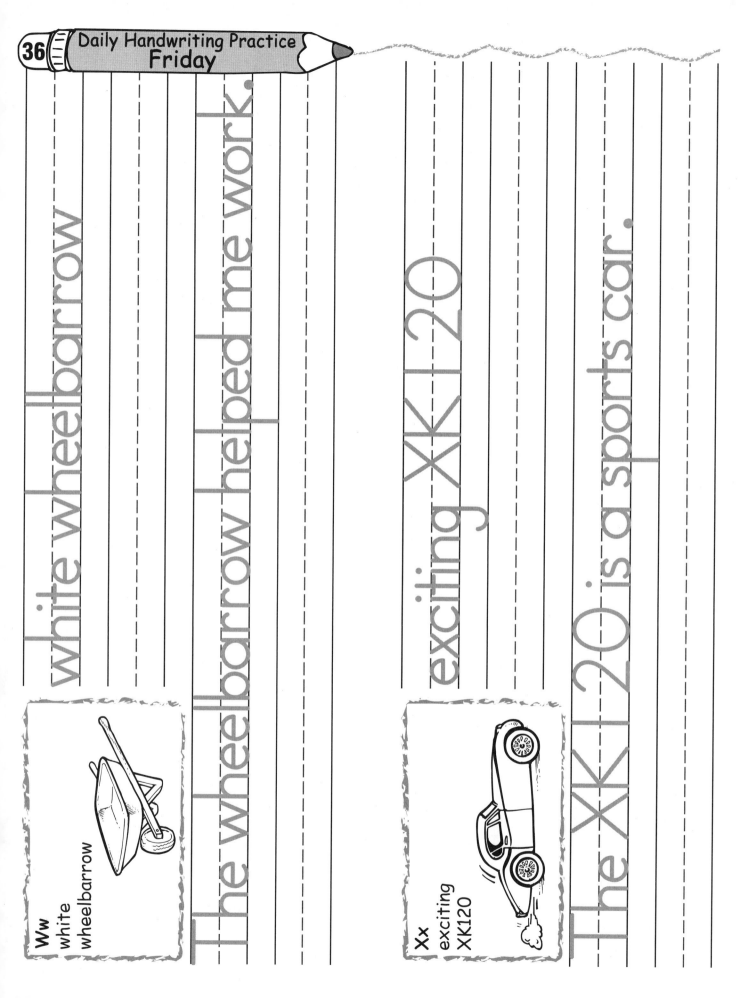

Ww
white
wheelbarrow

white wheelbarrow

The wheelbarrow helped me work.

Xx
exciting
XK120

exciting XK120

The XK120 is a sports car.

Yy
yellow
yacht

yellow yacht

Yvette yearns for the yellow yacht.

Zz
zooming
Zero

zooming Zero

The Zero was a real plane.

Teacher: Use pages 99–112 to create My Vehicle Alphabet Book for students to take home and share with their families. Staple the completed pages inside this cover.

fold

My Vehicle
Alphabet Book

This ABC Book of Vehicles represents my best handwriting.

I have practiced writing (and reading) all of the alphabet

in lots of different words.

My name is _____

I dedicate this book to _____